FOCUS ON OFFENDERS

The Key To Eliminating Domestic Violence

FOCUS ON OFFENDERS

The Key To Eliminating Domestic Violence

Kevin E. Reed

© *2013*

*This book is dedicated to Tamara, Khari and Amara.
I love you all tremendously.*

Table of Contents

Foreword 1

Preface 3

Chapter 1 **A Familiar Foe** 6

Chapter 2 **Focusing On Victims Has Hit Its Limits** 16

Chapter 3 **Reduce Domestic Violence Further By Focusing On Offenders** 38

Chapter 4 **Determining The Primary Offenders** 47

Chapter 5 **Targeting High Offenders** 69

Chapter 6 **Teen Dating Violence** 75

Chapter 7 **Reducing Recidivism** 78

Chapter 8 **Focus On Offenders** 91

Endnotes 94

About The Author 95

All of the events herein are true. Some names and details have been changed to protect privacy.

Foreword

My name is Lia Roemer and I work for the YWCA of Greater Memphis and the Blueprint for Safety Adaptation Demonstration Initiative. I started as a volunteer victim advocate for the YWCA and then became full-time in 2009. That same year I met Commissioner Reed at a planning session regarding protective orders. In that session we had to break in to small groups and discuss the highs and lows of working in domestic violence. Commissioner Reed and I were in the same group. I spoke about my role as a domestic violence advocate and how important it is to build a strong rapport with victims of intimate partner violence. When it was his turn, he talked in-depth about representing abusers as a public defender and seeing firsthand how they routinely manipulate the criminal justice system. He expressed a sincere hope that these batterers would change. I felt encouraged to find that he was very knowledgeable about domestic violence and that he spoke of batterers possibly being able to overcome their abusive ways.

I work on the frontline with victims of intimate partner violence, and it is clear to me that domestic violence is spreading. Unfortunately, the violence is accepted in our communities and has become part of our everyday life. It has gone beyond our homes and into our schools. It is in our music, our media, our places of worship and our jobs. It is our duty to look for ways to end domestic violence. Most importantly, we must stop blaming victims. I have spoken at many domestic violence events and the question still comes up. Why doesn't the victim just leave?

In this book Commissioner Reed discusses the benefits of focusing on offenders. He offers innovative theories and concrete actions that could have a major impact on reducing domestic violence. Why has the fight against domestic violence stalled? Why do we now need to focus on offenders? Can offenders truly be held accountable within the judicial system? Commissioner Reed offers insightful and thought provoking answers to these questions.

There is no quick fix to the domestic violence problem, but the ideas in this book give me hope that batterers can be compelled to stop being abusive. I encourage advocates, activists, lawyers, counselors, judges and all who are involved with intimate partner violence to read this book and start the discussion to bring about change.

-Lia Roemer, Advocacy Coordinator, YWCA of Greater Memphis and Blueprint for Safety Adaptation Demonstration Initiative

Preface

In January 2012 William Daye was charged with second-degree murder and domestic violence aggravated assault by the Memphis Police Department. According to the Affidavit of Complaint, Daye and his girlfriend, Rhonda Gavin, were fighting in the front yard of Daye's home. Ms. Gavin's brother, Joseph Gavin, arrived at Daye's home and saw Daye hitting his sister. He exited his vehicle and began to fight with Daye. Daye then ran into his home and came out with a semi-automatic pistol. By this time, the Gavins had gotten into Joseph's car. Daye came around to the driver's side and started firing through the window. Joseph Gavin was killed instantly.

As the magistrate on duty the evening that Daye was arrested, my task was to set bail for him. In making this determination it was brought to my attention that Daye was currently on probation for domestic assault, a misdemeanor in Shelby County, Tennessee. Originally, Daye had been arrested for the felony charge of domestic aggravated assault in July 2010, but he eventually pled guilty to the reduced charge of domestic assault and was placed on probation. My curiosity led me to retrieve the Affidavit of Complaint for the 2010 charge. What I read was chilling and sad.

In July 2010 Ms. Gavin was giving Daye a ride to his home when an argument erupted. When they got to Daye's home he exited the car and started firing shots at the vehicle while she was still inside. Daye then opened the door and struck her in the head with the gun. Members of Daye's family came to Ms. Gavin's rescue and pulled him off her. The police arrived, arrested Daye, and took pictures of Ms. Gavin's injuries, the bullet-riddled car, and the shell casings on the ground.

I could not believe what I was reading. Eighteen months earlier Daye had been arrested for shooting at Ms. Gavin while she was in her car in front of his home. The affidavits were so similar that I had to make sure I was reading the right one. Now her brother was dead, and I could not help but wonder why she was still in a relationship with Daye. Why would she have anything to do with a man that had shot at her? And how did his felony charge get reduced to a misdemeanor with all the eyewitnesses and physical evidence that was available? I had the uneasy feeling that Joseph Gavin's death did not have to happen.

There was one question, however, that was especially intriguing to me. Why was Daye still abusive? He had been arrested; he had pled guilty; and he had been placed on probation. But his violent behavior had not changed. He was still a deadly abuser. Yet my knee-jerk reaction was to wonder whether *Ms. Gavin* had somehow brought this on herself. As for Daye, I was not surprised to see that he had remained abusive after the 2010 arrest.

Something was wrong with my thought process. Why had I unconsciously assigned some of the blame to Ms. Gavin? Why did I immediately examine whether her actions had led to her brother's death? The reason, of course, is because we expect victims to do what is in the best interest of their safety, namely leave abusers. Often though, for a variety of reasons, they do not leave; and it is this decision made by thousands of victims everyday that has stalled the fight against domestic violence.

The abuse dynamics illustrated by Rhonda Gavin and William Daye lead to one unavoidable conclusion. If we want to eliminate domestic violence, we have to figure out how to get offenders to change. We have to somehow compel them to stop being abusive. The traditional solution of encouraging victims to leave abusers no longer resonates strongly with today's victims. It ignores an inconvenient truth; victims want to stay in their relationships. As a result, many of the tactics currently being used to fight domestic violence are not producing the desired results.

The goal of *Focus On Offenders* is to make the case that the fight against domestic violence now needs to focus some of its efforts on the source of the problem, offenders. I have attempted to illustrate with stories, examples, and data that by adding tactics which focus on offenders communities will begin to see a steady reduction in domestic violence. Additionally, I demonstrate exactly how to accomplish this and explain why I believe this method will work.

Hopefully, the information herein will prove to be compelling and useful.

The nature of domestic violence has changed over the years. As a result, our preventative tactics need to adapt as well. My hope is that this book will spark new debate and discussion among all stakeholders about how to further reduce and eventually eliminate domestic violence.

-Kevin E. Reed

1.

A Familiar Foe

Paper-thin Protection

When Vicki James appeared before me requesting an order of protection against her husband, Walter James, he was already in custody for pointing a gun at Vicki and threatening to shoot her. When I asked her my standard first question, "Why do you need an order of protection against Walter James?" she replied, "'cause I finally grew a spine." Vicki was petite in stature standing just over five feet. She looked like she weighed about 120 pounds. Her husband, wearing county-issued blue jail scrubs, was positioned in the hearing room about 15 feet from her in the lock-up area. He stood over six feet tall and looked to be about 200 pounds. Vicki's demeanor was feisty and determined as she stood before the court. Choosing to represent herself, she spoke with a rapid-fire pace looking directly at Walter when she talked about the abuse he inflicted. When she was not speaking she would often cut her eyes at her husband glaring at him with a look of pure disdain.

For his part Walter was mostly quiet during the hearing. During the most egregious parts of her testimony he would drop his eyes, shift his weight, shake his head from side to side, and mutter, "No, no" or "That's not true" just loud enough for Vicki and me to hear. Officially he chose to remain silent and did not offer a formal response to his wife's version of the incident.

Ms. James stated that her husband had relapsed and was using "meth" again. The methamphetamine caused his behavior to be erratic and they fought incessantly about his drug habit. What upset her most, though, was the constant flow of strangers who were now coming to the house, ostensibly to buy, sell, or use meth with her husband. Vicki had dealt with her husband's drug use in the past, and maybe Walter thought she would be just as accommodating now. For some reason, though, the drug traffic coming through her home was intolerable this time.

Vicki confronted Walter about all the strangers coming to the house to use drugs and an explosive argument erupted. The two launched into a yelling and screaming match that Vicki was determined not to lose. The verbal confrontation lasted nearly an hour when Walter decided he had taken enough. He went to their bedroom and retrieved a gun from his dresser drawer. As Vicki described the incident, Walter grabbed her by her neck, put the gun to her head, and raged repeatedly that he would kill her. She stated she was terrified because he had hit her in the past and was likely high on meth. In that moment she truly believed that he would kill her. She wrestled herself away from him, went to another room, and called the police. Upon finding out that Vicki had called the police, Walter gave the gun to their eight-year old son and ordered him to hide the weapon. When the police arrived Walter was arrested and charged with aggravated assault against his wife. Two weeks later, the two appeared in court on Vicki's petition for an order of protection. Walter was still in custody having not made bail of $50,000. In addition to the order of protection that Vicki was requesting, Walter had already been ordered not to have any contact with her as a condition of his bail should he make it.

If I never heard Walter James' name again this would be just another unfortunate, garden variety domestic violence incident; but what happened instead was the realization of Vicki's worst nightmare. Walter made bail after that hearing, and two days later he went to their home and shot his wife three times in the stomach in front of their children. This time Walter intended to make good on his threats.

The Affidavit of Complaint stated that Walter had come to the home demanding to be let in. Vicki refused. He then toggled the breaker switch on the house to the off position, cutting the power. Vicki, fearing for her life, called the police and Walter fled. Two hours later Walter came back to the house and kicked in the door. He was armed with a .22 caliber rifle and shot Vicki three times in the abdomen while their children were in the same room. He was still on the scene when the police arrived for the second time to find Vicki bleeding profusely from gunshot wounds and with lacerations on her head. Thankfully, Vicki survived the shooting. Walter was charged with attempted second-degree murder and his bail was set at $1,000,000.

For those of us who fight against domestic violence, men like Walter James represent a troubling group of offenders. He represents the type of offender that most believe is unreachable and unchangeable. Walter was going to control Vicki or kill her regardless of what she did to protect herself. As soon as he made bail his objective was to get back in the house despite being ordered to stay away. When she refused to let him in, he tried to kill her.

Some of my colleagues, after hearing what happened to Vicki, cynically commented that an order of protection was just a piece paper; and if a man truly wanted to kill his wife an order of protection was not going to stop him. I understood their sentiment, but also knew that was not always the case. I knew of countless instances where an order of protection had stopped the abuse and helped the victim; however, Walter James made the point hard to argue. In fact, Walter James made preventing domestic violence seem impossible.

Power, Control, And Cheating

Thankfully, the vast majority of abusers do not come in the form of the homicidal type like Walter James. Most victims have to deal with partners who are typically accusatory, mean, and controlling, like Bill Lassiter. Bill Lassiter was an extremely abusive husband. What made him frightening was his ability to inflict abuse on his wife in private and then turn his abusive behaviors off when others were around.

Bill was just as dangerous as Walter James. In many ways his actions were even more sinister than Walter's. Bill could inflict intense abuse on his wife without ever laying a hand on her. By abusing her in this way, he always avoided getting arrested whenever the police were called. During their marriage he inflicted severe emotional abuse on her, and after they separated he stalked her every move for years. He could have been the national poster child for stalking ex-husbands. He had deep emotional insecurities originating from his childhood; and as an adult he had a mistrustful and confrontational relationship with his parents. He had no idea how to receive love or reciprocate it. He had a hair trigger temper, and he was my client.

In some divorce cases you are way down the road of litigation before you realize your client is actually the problem spouse. By then, it is too late to do anything about it except see the case to the end as quickly as you can. This was not true with Bill Lassiter. From the moment he walked into my office, I knew Bill was trouble. He looked to be in his mid-twenties and was of medium stature. His angry demeanor and permanent scowl were so intense that he always looked ready to explode, particularly when discussing his divorce case. When my secretary called him into my office he came in, dragged my interview chair up to the front of my desk, sat down, opened his folder of notes, and stared at me. He did not utter a single word, as if I should have already known why he was there. Needless to say, I was taken aback.

In the years before I became a magistrate, I had a robust family law practice. Bill's wife Susan had filed for divorce against him, and Bill wanted me to represent him. The divorce per se was not an issue for Bill because he no longer wanted to be married to his wife. They had only been married for a short time. The marriage had been very rocky, and they had no assets to fight over. But they had a five-year old daughter who would be the object of intense fighting and litigation over the next year. Susan had managed to obtain a temporary injunction barring Bill from having any contact with their daughter. It was this injunction and subsequent custody fight that provided the backdrop for Susan's accusations of extreme verbal abuse, jealous rages, threats, stalking, and harassment by her husband.

In the divorce pleadings Susan did not allege that Bill had ever physically assaulted her. The abuse she complained about, which eventually forced her to flee their home, was intense, uncontrollable verbal abuse which Bill would unleash on her in front of their child. Bill constantly accused her of cheating on him. During his rants he would call her a whore, slut, or bitch while demanding to know whom she was sleeping with. Whenever Susan mentioned divorce he would threaten to take their child from her if she ever actually filed. After enduring Bill's behavior for three years, Susan finally presented him with divorce papers. He immediately kicked her out of the house and canceled her bank card, cutting off all access to funds.

Susan's divorce papers contained an unexpected surprise, however. She and her lawyer had convinced the judge to grant her temporary custody of their daughter as a part of the initial divorce complaint. In other words, at the same time sheriff deputies were serving Bill with divorce papers, they were also handing over his daughter to Susan. In addition, Susan had obtained a temporary injunction barring Bill from coming around her or the child until a hearing could be held. Susan had landed two knockout blows right at the onset of the custody fight, even before Bill knew there was a custody fight.

I would imagine that many abuse victims have to deal with offenders who are calculating with their abuse, like Bill. Bill was the type of offender who emotionally terrorized and threatened his victim in an attempt to control her actions, but rarely did anything that would lead to his arrest. In fact, Susan had called the police on many occasions complaining that Bill's temper and verbal raging had placed her in fear for her life. The police would come, but never arrest him. By the time they arrived Bill would be calm and cooperative.

Despite the allegations of verbal abuse, I managed to obtain some visitation time for Bill and his daughter. Bill had visitation from Thursday morning to Sunday evening every other weekend. He got to see his daughter from Tuesday morning to Wednesday morning during the weeks when he did not have weekend visitation. This was an incredible amount of visitation time considering the circumstances.

But Bill's anger with Susan for leaving him and obtaining primary custody could not be contained. Nearly every exchange of the child was problematic. If Susan was more than five minutes late to the drop-off location Bill would leave with the child and make Susan drive across town to retrieve her. If she was there early, he would call her derogatory names or complain about her lack of parenting skills whenever the child was in her care. He was convinced that Susan was never home when the child was with her and that her mother actually took care of the child while Susan was out partying. This belief formed Bill's basis for driving past Susan's home to see if her car was there in order to "gather evidence" of her negligent parenting skills. Despite my admonishments to stop driving past her house, Bill wanted Susan to see him out there, so he kept doing it.

One particularly alarming exchange caused Bill's visitation time to be completely suspended. Their daughter had become sick while in Bill's care. Susan carried the child's health insurance, but she had refused to give Bill the health insurance card for fear that he would discover where she worked and harass her on the job. Bill felt that Susan was deliberately trying to make him incur unnecessary medical expenses and did not take the child to the doctor. On the day of the exchange, Bill left the child in his car as he verbally attacked Susan. Susan engaged Bill in a heated argument. Susan's mother, who always accompanied her daughter for these exchanges, joined in the fight. Then Susan's mother went to Bill's car and took the child out of the car. Bill exploded. He threatened to kill Susan's mother if she ever went in his car again. He then got into his vehicle and erratically drove it toward Susan, nearly striking her. When the judge heard about this incident he took away all of Bill's visitation time until he could make a final determination of the custody matters at the divorce trial.

To my shock and amazement the trial provided the occasion for one last act of aggression on Bill's part. Even though Bill knew the judge had already formed a negative opinion of him, he still wanted his day in court to see if he could convince the judge to give him primary custody of their daughter. On the stand Bill denied all the abuse allegations. He stated to the judge that he and his wife did have emotional arguments, but only because she was cheating on him. We were even able to show through phone records that Susan did have a secret relationship with a police officer, although she claimed the relationship was platonic in nature. The only time I ever saw Bill look pleased was when Susan sheepishly admitted that she had exercised with a male police officer without her husband's knowledge. From that admission Bill gleaned a tiny bit of justification.

In the end, Bill's temper and behavior were too much to overcome. I knew that our cause was lost before the trial started, but Bill apparently still held out hope. As soon as the judge uttered that he was giving Susan primary custody of their child and keeping Bill's suspension in place, he abruptly jumped up from his seat, stormed out of the courtroom, and left the courthouse. The judge was shocked to see Bill get up and leave during the delivery of his verdict. The court went on high security alert as sheriff deputies searched the building and the parking lot for Bill. He was surely going to be held in contempt and placed in jail, but they could not find him. I was ordered to summon him back to the courtroom, but he would not answer his phone. I was completely outdone and embarrassed. Susan and her lawyer were mortified. The general consensus by all in attendance was that Bill Lassiter was a powder keg who needed to learn to control his temper before he could spend time with his child. Now, to make matters worse for Bill, he was going to have to convince this same judge that he had changed before visitation would be allowed again. I had no idea how he planned to do that.

Shortly thereafter I concluded my representation of Bill Lassiter. Our relationship ended with his situation being exactly the same as it was when he first walked into my office a year earlier, no contact with his daughter or Susan. But he was now divorced.

Interestingly enough, I saw the Lassiters again seven years later. Susan and Bill appeared before me as a magistrate on her petition for an order of protection against him. It was surreal to see them standing in the same room together so many years later. I could not hear the petition, of course, because of my prior relationship with the Lassiters, but I was dismayed to see that their problems persisted seven years after the divorce. I chose not to read the allegations in

Susan's petition. I did not want to confirm that Bill was still harassing her.

Marion's Secret

On August 23, 2011 there was a domestic homicide in Marion, Arkansas. Kristin Andrews shot and killed her husband, Stanley Andrews, during a fight in their home. They had been married for 10 years. The murder had plenty of scintillating and sensational details which helped keep the incident in the local news for months. Kristin had shot her husband in the presence of their three children and then called 911 to report the murder. She happened to be the daughter of a high-ranking sheriff in that same county. Even though the murder had been reported at 8:48 pm, Stanley's mother was not notified until the morning of the following day. At her arraignment Kristin received a very low bail of $5,000 and was quickly freed. The judge refused to give a comment about the bail amount, but the victim's family was livid and vocal. They accused the judge of giving Kristin preferential treatment because of her father's relationship with the court.

Additionally, there were conflicting reports about whether there had been any prior incidents of domestic altercations between the two. One news station reported that the local police had no record of prior domestic incidents, while another news station reported that the police had gone to the couple's home the Saturday prior to the murder to settle a dispute over car keys. Stanley's mother stated she was unaware that her son and his wife were having any marital issues. She had just seen the wife recently and everything seemed fine.

The comments sections of the online reports on the incident quickly filled up with statements by anonymous posters passing judgments on the situation. "Cold-blooded murderer", "Battered spouse," and the occasional "Let's see what the evidence turns up" were the categories of most of the comments. However, something else altogether about this murder captured my attention, something that seemed incredible to me and somewhat hard to believe. Prior to the Andrews murder, the last time there had been a murder in Marion was nearly 20 years earlier!

It was the first thing that was reported by the media after news of the murder broke. You would have to go back nearly 20 years to find the last time someone was killed in Marion, Arkansas. Some of Marion's citizens appeared on the news expressing shock and disbelief that anything like this could happen in their town. I thought it was one of the most amazing crime statistics I had ever heard.

I thought about how wonderful it would be if my hometown of Memphis, Tennessee could go just one year without a domestic violence fatality. Memphis had averaged 22 domestic homicides per year over the last 14 years. Marion had only one homicide of any type - Stanley Andrews. Of course, it is not exactly an apples-to-apples comparison. Although they are separated by just 12 miles, Marion is a small town with a population of about 12,000 people. Memphis is an urban city with a population of over 600,000 people. It is certainly true where there are less people there is less conflict, but a run of nearly 20 years between murders was impressive even for a small town. Marion's success made me wonder if it was possible for an urban community to go one year or more without a domestic homicide. Could Marion's small town success translate to large cities? How do you prevent domestic homicides in cities with hundreds of thousands or even millions of people? Was there truly a way to combat crimes of passion that happen in the heat of the moment between intimate partners? How do you stop potentially fatal abuse happening in the privacy of people's homes?

Obviously, these were difficult questions to answer with any certainty. I did know this much to be true - the only way to stop domestic homicides was to stop domestic violence in general. You could not expect to stop domestic homicides without tackling the larger problem of domestic violence. Conversely, if a community was vigorously fighting domestic violence, then it was also vigorously fighting domestic homicides at the same time.

So the real question is can urban communities reduce domestic violence so significantly that the number of domestic homicides drops to zero? If the answer to this question is yes, then domestic homicides in large cities could be prevented.

2.

Focusing On Victims

Has Hit Its Limits

Slow Progress... Then No Progress

The strategies developed over the past 35 years to fight domestic homicide in America have produced positive results, but success did not come quickly.

Starting in the mid-1970s the plight of women suffering through often fatal violence perpetrated by their male partners was pushed to the very forefront of our national public conscience. The general strategy of the anti-domestic violence movement was to bring attention to, condemn, and punish men who abused their wives or girlfriends and to provide all manner of support for victims abused by these men.

Domestic violence activists made sure that everyone had a vital and immediate role to play in ending abuse. Lawmakers in state governments and in Congress enacted tougher domestic violence laws and elevated the seriousness of abuse. Law enforcement officers were encouraged and eventually mandated to determine and arrest the primary aggressor upon arriving at the scene of a domestic incident. The judiciary developed specialized domestic violence courts to deal specifically with offenders and related issues. Advocacy organizations developed programs and support groups for victims. Marketing firms created compelling public service announcements encouraging women in violent relationships to leave their abusers. Even Hollywood played a significant role by producing movies which exposed domestic violence as a terrifying ordeal that can happen to any woman without discrimination.

On the local level, activists sought to change police policy in favor of arresting more offenders and pushed for more severe punishments in court. They opened more shelters for battered women, developed hotlines with 24-hour access to help, offered assistance through the protective order process, and opened safety centers for centralized service for victims. They even sought to deal with the source of the problem by encouraging courts to send abusers to batterer intervention programs.

Galvanized by national statistics showing that over 80 percent of domestic violence victims were women, the movement's message was undeniable; an alarming number of women were being abused and victimized by their intimate partner, and society needed to do everything it could to help these women escape abusive relationships. Ultimately, activists sought to change the nation's attitude toward domestic violence from ambivalence to condemnation, and they were successful in doing so. As a result of their efforts, domestic violence against women began to slowly decline.

Domestic Violence By The Numbers

In 1993 the U.S. Department of Justice (DOJ) started publishing national data on the number of people who were criminally victimized by their intimate partner. The DOJ tallied the number of reported crimes perpetrated by intimate partners and expressed that value as a rate. In the case of female victims, the rate measured the number of victims per 1,000 persons age 12 or older who experienced violence from an intimate partner. The rate is our best estimate of the amount of intimate partner violence that is occurring nationally.

When you track the rate from 1993 to 2002, a 10-year period, you see a slow but steady decline of intimate partner violence against women. During this time period the victimization rate decreased by over 57 percent from 9.8 to 4.2.

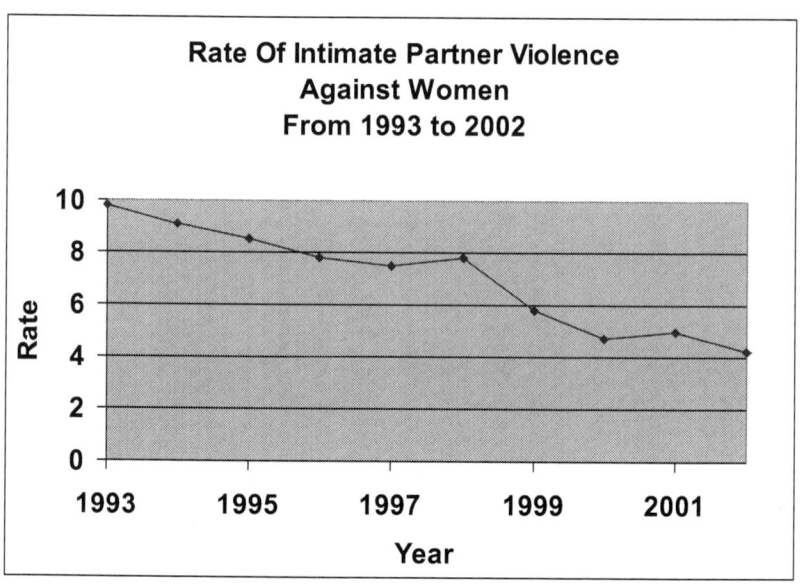

If this pace of decline could have been maintained it would have taken only another seven years for the victimization rate for women to begin to approach zero; but the decline did not continue. In fact, after 2002 the victimization rate remained virtually the same for the next seven years. In 2002 and 2009 the rate of women who had experienced violence from an intimate partner was the same, suggesting that progress had stalled during this time period. Then in 2010 the rate decreased to 3.1 where it remains today. From a national perspective, the fight to stop intimate partner violence against women hit a seven-year plateau before measureable gains would be seen again.

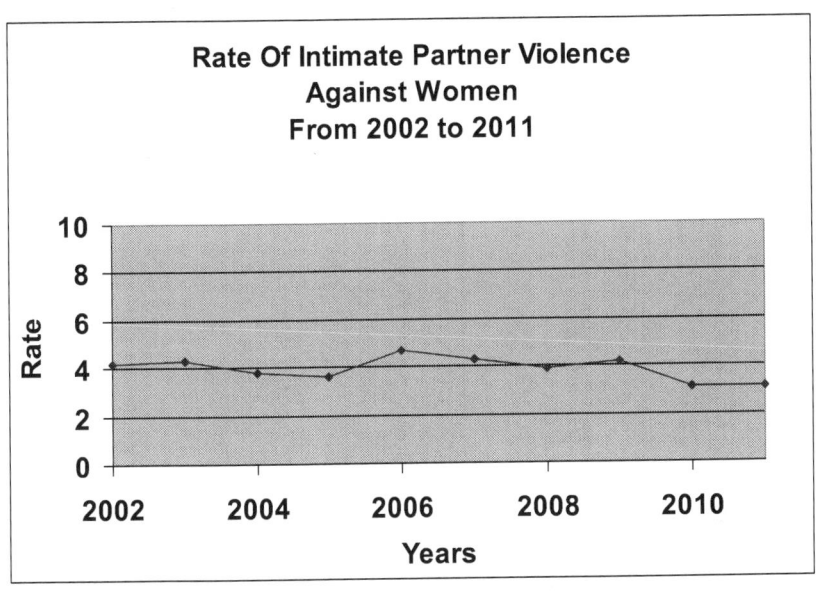

In contrast, the rate of intimate partner violence against men has remained consistently low since 1993. In 2011 the victimization rate for men was 0.8.

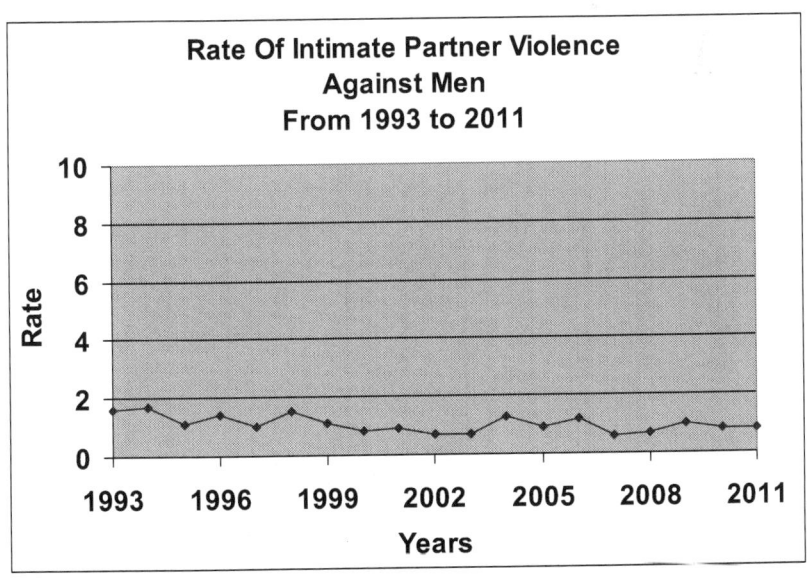

In 2010 the DOJ estimated there were 407,700 female victims of intimate partner violence and 101,530 male victims of intimate partner violence. In other words, eight out of every ten victims of intimate partner violence in the U.S. were women. Also in 2010, the National Center for Injury Prevention and Control published its National Intimate Partner and Sexual Violence Survey. The survey estimated that more than one-third of women (35.6 percent or approximately 42.4 million) had experienced rape, physical violence, and/or stalking by an intimate partner at some point in their lifetime. As for men, more than one in four (28.5 percent or approximately 32.3 million) had experienced rape, physical violence, and/or stalking by an intimate partner at some point in their lifetime.

An Unexpected Lack Of Cooperation

Something unexpected happened around 2002. The anti-domestic violence movement encountered a problem so severe that there would be no further decline of intimate partner domestic violence against women for the next seven years. The strategies and tactics being used to fight domestic violence were no longer producing the desired results. Not only that, activists seemed to have a difficult time figuring out how to restart progress.

For me the problem was obvious. As a young lawyer, I saw the evidence of the dilemma everyday. Victims were no longer cooperating with efforts designed to protect them. The movement's principle mantra - victims should leave their abuser for their own safety - seemed to be falling on deaf ears. A significant number of victims were not leaving their abuser at all. In the cases where victims did leave, it was only after suffering through many years of abuse. The reluctance of victims to leave their abuser manifested as an incredibly challenging problem that single-handedly stalled anti-domestic violence progress.

Defending Abusers

I first experienced the harsh realities associated with domestic violence while working as an Assistant Public Defender in Shelby County, Tennessee. Before then I knew very little about domestic violence, other than it was wrong. Because of this, my initial education came by way of defending those accused of domestic violence. Through my job as a public defender, I quickly learned to view domestic violence charges in the same way my clients viewed domestic violence charges - no victim, no case. My clients knew and I quickly discovered that domestic violence cases were the easiest cases to get dismissed because victims rarely followed through with prosecuting. They knew if the victim did not come to court, there would be no case.

I thoroughly enjoyed working as a public defender. There was no better place to work in terms of getting quality courtroom experience. You could move up to handling serious felonies as fast as your skills allowed. Over the course of time, I represented thousands of defendants on everything from trespassing to capital murder.

The assignment I enjoyed the most, however, was working on the felony preliminary hearing team. The six public defenders assigned to this team represented all the defendants who were charged with a felony up to the preliminary hearing stage of the criminal process. Most of the time we were able to work out plea deals with prosecutors, but when we could not, we scheduled preliminary hearings for our clients.

At a preliminary hearing the state is required to present some of its evidence to show that it has probable cause to substantiate the charges against the defendant. If probable cause exists, the defendant's case is sent to the grand jury to be considered for indictment and the criminal process continues. If probable cause does not exist, the charges are dismissed. Because probable cause is such a low evidentiary threshold, the vast majority of the cases set for preliminary hearing proceed to indictment.

This was not the case when the defendant was charged with a felony domestic violence offense - usually aggravated assault. These cases all hinged on one question, whether the victim was going to be present for the preliminary hearing. If he or she appeared, probable cause would be found and the case would be sent to the grand jury.

If he or she did not appear, the case would be dismissed. More often than not, the victim did not appear, and most of my domestic violence cases were dismissed.

Domestic violence is unlike any other type of criminal offense. It is the only criminal charge where the victim may not want to see the offender punished for his or her crime. With every other type of crime – theft, burglary, murder, vehicular assault, sexual assault, identity theft – the victim (or the victim's family in the case of murder) wants the offender to be punished for the crime and will happily assist in the prosecution. This is not the case with domestic violence. In domestic violence cases a cooperating victim is a pleasant surprise for prosecutors.

To really understand how unusual and different domestic violence cases are you have to go inside the interview room with the defendant. Normally, when a felony case was assigned to me I would go to the jail to conduct my initial interview with the client. In the public defender's office all the clients were indigent and most did not have the financial resources to make bail, particularly those charged with a felony. So I had to make daily trips to the jail to speak with clients. The jailers would bring my client into a small room containing only a plastic table and a few plastic chairs. During the initial interview, I would introduce myself, explain the charges and the criminal process, and then dive into the facts of the case. I would read the Affidavit of Complaint and then ask the defendant to tell me his or her version of events. From there we would begin to build a theory of defense. We might put together a list of potential witnesses who could support the defendant's version of events, or we might decide to gather additional physical evidence or records that could support the defendant. We might decide to challenge an illegal search or a wrongfully obtained statement, or we might even decide that the best course of action to take after looking at the facts and the law was to try to negotiate the best possible plea deal. In nearly all the cases I handled the decisions as to which courses of action to take depended on the evidence and what we felt we could prove or disprove.

This was not the case when the defendant was charged with felony domestic violence. With my domestic violence cases there was rarely a discussion about the facts, or potential witnesses, or any other evidence that might prove useful. After reading the Affidavit of Complaint nearly every defendant would say to me, "Set it for a hearing. She's not coming." And that would be the end of the interview. Most of these men were charged with aggravated assault, which meant they were accused of threatening or assaulting their intimate partner with something other than their hands. Sometimes it was a piece of furniture or usually just the closest hard item within reach. Sometimes it was a knife, but often it was a gun. A conviction for aggravated assault carried a possible punishment of at least three years in jail, yet the instruction from almost every defendant was the same, "Set it for a hearing. She's not coming."

The only question my clients would ask was whether their girlfriend or spouse would get in any trouble if they failed to show for the hearing after being subpoenaed. I knew they were asking this question on behalf of the victim with whom they were already in contact. My answer was always the same, "It's possible, but not likely." I knew that the state rarely arrested victims for failing to show for court and I understood why. If the prosecutor's office had a general policy of arresting women who failed to show for court, word of this would eventually get out in the community. Victims would not respond by coming to court, they would stop calling the police during a crisis. Additionally, the prosecutor's office would be accused of re-victimizing women who had already been abused. It was a slippery slope that served to benefit the defendant.

Sometimes I would even get calls from victims asking me the same question, "Will I go to jail if I don't come to court?" Again I would tell them the same thing, "It's possible, but not likely." Many would tell me they were going to dodge the subpoena so they could not be compelled to come to court. I offered no advice one way or the other on this course of action, telling them only that it was their decision to make. Admittedly, I never talked to any victim for longer than five minutes, but I never got the impression that any of them were under duress from the defendant when they called me. I surmised, however, that from jail the defendant had contacted the victim and turned on the charm, apologizing and promising to never be abusive again. Maybe it took a few phone calls from the defendant to convince the victim not to come to court, but those calls often worked, and even subpoenaed victims ignored orders to appear in court.

Occasionally, if the defendant's abuse was really egregious or he had numerous prior arrests for domestic violence, the state would issue a warrant for the arrest of the victim if she failed to show after being subpoenaed. The victim would get arrested, spend the night in jail, and then be brought to court to testify the next day. At the hearing she would reluctantly recount the abuse at the hands of the defendant and reluctantly point him out as if she was having a hard time recognizing him. I would then ask some questions that usually only served to bring out more details of the abuse. The judge would then find probable cause, the case would be sent to the grand jury for an indictment, and the defendant would remain in jail on the charge. Finally, the victim would be released and allowed to go home, most likely feeling that her interests had not been served.

Working in the domestic violence unit (DV) was a tough assignment for prosecutors. Most of the DV prosecutors that I knew hated it. Their disdain for domestic violence cases usually grew out of an inability to do what came naturally for them – prosecute wrongdoers. Prosecutors want to punish people who commit crimes and help those who have been victimized by crime. Usually victims welcome their help and do whatever they can to assist in the prosecution of the case. With domestic violence cases it was a toss-up as to whether the victim was going to cooperate or not. After a while, ambivalence would start to set in.

On any typical day while I was on the felony team, I would have three or four hearings scheduled for that morning and one would likely be a domestic violence felony. The only question I would ask the DV prosecutor was whether or not he or she had a victim for the hearing. If the answer was no, I knew I would be moving to dismiss the charges and my client would get out of jail. If the answer was yes, I knew the hearing would go forward and regardless of what I managed to prove, probable cause would be found and my client would remain in jail.

One DV prosecutor once boasted to me that if he had a victim he could win the hearing by just asking the victim four questions: What's your name? What happened to you on the date of the incident? Do you see the person who did this to you in the courtroom? Did all these events happen in Shelby County? Upon asking these four questions, he would then pass the witness to me. I would ask some questions aimed at suggesting the victim was not remembering the incident correctly; but in the end, the court would find probable cause and send the case to the grand jury.

Although I knew that domestic violence preliminary hearings were decided based on whether the victim appeared or not, it was still shocking to actually hear a judge say as much from the bench. I was handling a rather high-profile domestic violence case involving a state politician and her boyfriend. My client, the boyfriend, had been arrested several times in the past for assaulting the Assemblywoman, but she was notorious for bailing him out of jail after the arrest. Later, she would use her influence to have the charges dismissed or reduced. On this particular incident, he had threatened her with a knife causing him to be arrested again and charged with aggravated assault. On the day before the hearing, the DV prosecutor just happened to walk into the courtroom while I was in there. Upon seeing the prosecutor, the judge stopped what he was doing and specifically asked the prosecutor whether the Assemblywoman was definitely going to be in court the following day. The judge then said, "I don't want to be on TV tomorrow dismissing her case." The prosecutor told the judge that as far as he knew she was going to appear and testify. I am not sure if the judge knew I was in the courtroom listening to this exchange, but I am sure it would not have mattered to him either way. If the Assemblywoman appeared for the hearing the case was going to the grand jury. If she did not appear the case would be dismissed, and everybody understood this. On the following day, the Assemblywoman did appear for the hearing. She testified consistently with the Affidavit of Complaint, and her boyfriend remained in jail.

Making The Case Without A Victim

After I became a magistrate I had the opportunity to attend a state-wide domestic violence conference for prosecutors. Attending the conference were approximately 100 prosecutors and several members of the judiciary. The subject of uncooperative victims was a hot topic at the conference. It must have been a common issue for DV prosecutors across the state because one of the presentations focused on how to prosecute domestic violence cases without a victim.

The presenter discussed some rather complex legal maneuvers that prosecutors could try in order to avoid dismissal of their cases. The presenter tried to teach his colleagues how to use the hearsay exception *Forfeiture By Wrongdoing*. In general, the exception allows someone else to relate what the victim said if the defendant somehow kept the victim from appearing in court. For example, a police officer at the scene of the incident would be allowed to relate to the court what the victim said if it could be shown that the defendant convinced her not to come to court. It is a powerful exception, but difficult to use. Prosecutors are usually unable to prove the defendant is somehow manipulating the victim's appearance, even though that is often the case. Most of the time only the victim knows what the defendant is doing to keep her away from court. But if the prosecutor has the victim in order to prove manipulation, he obviously does not need to use the exception.

During the many years that I handled hundreds of felony domestic violence cases, I only had one preliminary hearing where probable cause was found without the victim being present. Needless to say, the defendant and I were shocked and surprised when it happened. The prosecutor used the *Excited Utterance* hearsay exception to get statements made by the victim admitted even though she did not appear in court.

The victim in the case had been brutally assaulted and held against her will in her boyfriend's home for several days. During the ordeal the victim had been tied up, whipped repeatedly, and was not allowed to leave or use the phone. In the evenings he would unbind her, but whenever he left during the day he would tie her up again until he returned. On the third day the victim escaped. He had tied her up before he left, but she got loose and ran out of the house. She ran to a neighbor's home half-dressed, bruised, lacerated, crying uncontrollably, and frantic. She told the neighbor what her boyfriend had done to her over the past three days and begged her to call the police. Shortly thereafter, the boyfriend was arrested and charged with especially aggravated kidnapping and especially aggravated assault. His case was assigned to me.

At the hearing the prosecutor informed me that she was unable to find the victim and therefore could not serve her with a subpoena. She intended to go forward with the hearing using the neighbor to introduce what the victim said. I did not think the maneuver would work. After all, the right to confront your accuser is a well-established constitutional right. At the hearing I moved to dismiss the case telling the court that the state had no victim and that any statements attributed to the victim from the neighbor would be inadmissible hearsay. The prosecutor responded by telling the court that she could use the *Excited Utterance* exception to get the statements admitted. The prosecutor argued to the court that the victim told the neighbor exactly what her boyfriend did to her and the neighbor knew my client was the victim's boyfriend. Most importantly, the victim had made these statements to the neighbor while she was visibly distraught, terrified, and still in distress from the ordeal, thereby qualifying as excited utterances. The judge agreed.

The neighbor, an elderly woman who looked to be in her late 70s, was small in stature and quite frail, but she did not appear to be intimidated by the proceeding. She related to the court how the victim came to her house beating on the door and screaming for help. She said the victim immediately told her that the defendant had beaten her, tied her up for days, and would not let her leave his home. She related that the victim's face and wrists were bruised and that she had welts on her stomach and back. She tried to comfort the victim and calm her down, but the victim would not stop crying. By the time the police arrived the victim was still visibly shaken. She was able to tell the police where to find her boyfriend, and he was arrested that same hour.

As it turned out, the boyfriend was the one who owned the house and lived next door to the neighbor. The victim was apparently a new girlfriend who was new to the neighborhood. The neighbor had seen the victim going in and out of the boyfriend's home on a few occasions, but they never had a conversation until that day; and they never had another conversation after that day. In fact, the neighbor had not seen or heard from the victim since the incident occurred. She had no information as to her whereabouts.

I drilled the neighbor on her accuracy and her memory, but as usual my questions only served to bring out more details of the horrific event. In the end, the neighbor's testimony was more than enough evidence to keep my client in jail even without the victim. The defendant was shocked when he realized that he would not be getting out of jail that day. I tried to explain the law to him, but he was in no mood for a lesson on the rules of evidence. For once, no victim - no case had failed.

An Escape Plan Fails

You do not have to work in the domestic violence field to know that victims are reluctant to leave abusers. Anyone who has ever tried to help a victim escape domestic violence can attest to the perplexing behavior of victims who stay with an abuser. The reasons victims do not leave are numerous, complex, and completely valid. Some of the more common reasons are fear of retaliation from the abuser, lack of housing support, lack of financial support, not wanting to be dependent on others, fear of losing custody of the children, hoping the abuser will change, being isolated from family and friends, religious and cultural stigmas, low self-esteem, embarrassment and shame, and love for the abuser.

Still, even when you understand victim psychology, it can be a frustrating and heartbreaking experience to see a friend or loved one choose to stay with an abuser. I had an experience where I was sure I had helped a good friend finally escape her abuser. I was wrong.

The voicemail I received was from Janet Givens, the mother of one of my best friends, Steve. Steve was living and working in London at the time of his mother's crisis. I do not know if Ms. Givens called me because she knew I worked in the domestic violence field or if she simply had no one else local to call. Her voicemail indicated that her husband was drinking again, his abusive behaviors had returned, and she had grown tired of his abuse. She was contemplating leaving him. I immediately called Steve to alert him to his mother's distress and to get more information about her relationship with her husband.

Steve told me his mother's husband had a history of alcoholism and he was physically and verbally abusive to her when he drank. He had insisted several times that she leave him, telling her she did not have to put up with that type of behavior. She responded by telling Steve that when her husband was not drinking he was fine, and when he was drinking she knew what to do in order to keep him from going off. In fact, the crisis this time was in large part because her husband had not drank in a very long time, allowing Ms. Givens to enjoy an extended period of peace in the home. Then he had a drink while they were out one evening with friends. He told her that he could handle the alcohol in moderation, but over time his abusive behaviors slowly returned. The thought of once again dealing with her husband's abuse was too much for Ms. Givens to handle. This time she was prepared to leave.

Her phone call to me was to let me know she was going to leave her husband very shortly and she might need my help to make the transition. She wanted to save up a little more money and then she was leaving. I assured her that she had a place to stay when she got ready to leave, and we talked about foregoing financial considerations if her husband became violent. She told me she felt certain that she could manage the situation for a little while longer. She was secretly packing when he was not home and saving money from her paycheck.

I did not expect to get the phone call I received a couple of weeks later. Ms. Givens was calling me from jail. She had been arrested for domestic assault and needed someone to pick her up.

Ms. Givens had been jailed the previous evening. She said her husband had started arguing with her again, although she never disclosed what the argument was about. During the altercation her husband slapped a glass of milk out of her hand. At that point Ms. Givens snapped and physically attacked him. She did not say how long the fight lasted, but when it ended Ms. Givens called the police thinking that her husband would be arrested and taken to jail. When the officers arrived, however, they found Ms. Givens to be hysterical, irate, and uncontrollable. They found her husband to be calm, cool, and not drunk. They determined that she was the primary aggressor and charged her with domestic assault.

Interestingly enough, Ms. Givens told me later that she was extremely embarrassed by the situation and initially had no intentions of calling me; but her husband had made her bail and was now waiting outside the jail to take her home. She had nothing but the clothes on her back, but she was determined not to go back to her home ever again. The carefully planned escape she was secretly orchestrating had fallen apart; but as far as she was concerned, this was just the push she needed to leave her husband for good.

Over the next few months Ms. Givens made plans to join her son in Europe. She was not able to leave immediately because she had to get a passport and make court appearances. Before she left town she made several police escorted trips to her home to gather her personal belongings. She had managed to save enough money to rent a car so she could get around and put her affairs in order before leaving. Her lawyer was able to convince the prosecutor to set the case off for one year. If there were no further problems, Ms. Givens' case would be dismissed.

The most difficult thing Ms. Givens had to do was resign from her job. Her job was a source of strength for her. Working boosted her self-esteem and allowed her daily respite from her problems at home. She liked having her own money, but more importantly she felt independent and useful. She had delayed leaving her abusive husband because she knew that leaving him meant leaving town and thus leaving her job. She tried to continue working for a little while after her arrest, but her husband kept coming to the job trying to speak with her. It was a dangerous situation for Ms. Givens and her co-workers because he knew where she was for eight hours of the day and was intent on convincing her to come home. She felt it best to resign, but she hated having to do so.

Her husband constantly tried to communicate with her after she left the home. He waited for her after work. He waited for her after court. He called her on the phone and sent text messages and emails. He desperately tried to get Ms. Givens to come home. He promised to be on his best behavior, but Ms. Givens was unmoved. She had left for good, and now she had an opportunity to start a new life in a new country with her son.

She lived with me until her case was resolved, then she moved in with her sister who lived in Arkansas. After her passport arrived she left for London. Her arrest for domestic assault had obviously not been part of her escape plan, but in hindsight she might have still been in the home saving money and waiting for the right time to leave if not for the altercation. Her escape was delayed due to her arrest, but she had successfully left her abuser with the help of family and friends.

After Ms. Givens arrived in London I reflected on how uncommonly lucky she was. It took some time and an unfortunate arrest, but she had finally left a man who had been abusing her for years. Although her husband had alienated her from most of her relatives and friends that lived nearby, she still was able to call on other friends who were willing to help in her time of need. She had prepared to leave by saving up money, which gave her the ability to obtain transportation during the transition. The money she saved meant she did not have to rely on her husband for basic needs as long as someone could provide shelter for her. She had a son who was capable and willing to take her in for as long as she needed. Additionally, she did not have any minor children to consider. She did not have to deal with the crippling decision of whether to separate the children from their father, their friends, their school, and their activities; nor did she have to deal with the intense and often violent backlash from an abuser when his children are taken away. If any one of these factors had been different, Ms. Givens might not have decided to leave. She was fortunate to have the support she needed at the time she needed it. In my mind, Ms. Givens was no longer a victim; she was a survivor.

With all this going for her, you can imagine my surprise when I learned from her son that Ms. Givens had returned to her husband after four months in London. Steve was not going to tell me either. During a conversation about something entirely different, I casually asked how his mother was doing. He reluctantly told me that she was back in Memphis. He could not bring himself to say back in Memphis with her husband; but I knew she had no other place to go in Memphis if not with me. Unable to find employment that could support her in London, Ms. Givens had returned to her husband because she did not like feeling dependent on others. It did not matter that the "others" were her son and daughter-in-law who begged her to stay. She had no money of her own, no prospects of a good job, and now all of the things she left behind loomed large in her mind. All her world was in Memphis, and if reclaiming her world meant going back to her abusive husband, she would accept that. Making the return easier, of course, were her husband's promises to treat her better and to never drink again.

It was a sobering reality check. Ms. Givens had escaped her husband and literally moved to another country; but after six months away, she returned to her abuser. I tried to comfort my friend by telling him that victims try to leave many, many times before they finally break free from their abuser and he should not give up on his mother. I told him that we should both continue to check on her, be concerned for her safety, and be ready to assist again if she tried to leave him in the future. He agreed, but the disappointment was still there.

With all my training and years working in the domestic violence field the best advice I could give my friend was to be ready to assist again *if* his mother tried to leave again. I recognized immediately that this was really no advice at all. Of course he was going to help his mother escape her abuser as many times as it took. But what could be done to help protect her now while she was back in the home?

I had another feeling about the situation, one that I did not expect to feel - resignation. I knew my best friend also felt resignation about his mother's situation after she returned to Memphis. Years earlier he had distanced himself mentally from the realities of his mother's relationship as a coping mechanism for himself. Then, when the opportunity of escape presented itself, he was ready with unlimited support to help free her. Now she was back in the same situation. I could hear the disappointment and resignation in his voice and I understood why he had those feelings, because I had them too. The knee-jerk reaction was to feel like I had done what I could for Ms. Givens. Now she was on her own. She was an intelligent woman capable of making her own choices, and she had chosen the abuser over her personal safety. What more could be done?

Clearly those thoughts were wrong, but I had to beat those feelings back more than once. I knew I had to keep checking on her regularly while she was in Memphis, and I knew I had to be ready to help her escape again no matter how many times it took.

Nowhere To Escape To
It is hard to say what the most prevalent reason is as to why victims do not leave abusers. Not having a place to escape to, even if they tried to leave, would likely rank near the top. In stark contrast to the support Ms. Givens had, many victims have no one to call on for help and no place to go for shelter in order to escape an abuser. The lack of an alternative place of safety often forces victims to repeatedly subject themselves to abuse.

This was the unfortunate reality of Trini Baker. Trini described to me an ordeal with her boyfriend that clearly illustrated the precarious nature of the situation she was in. Trini was estranged from her family and was living with her boyfriend and his family. One evening her boyfriend came home from work and wanted to have sex with her. Generally, this would not have been a problem, but on this evening she was not feeling well and refused his advances. He then became irate and tried to force himself on her, but she continued to resist him both physically and verbally. Finally he gave up, but not before slapping her repeatedly and calling her demeaning and derogatory names.

The next day she told a friend about what happened during the night. Her friend told her that what her boyfriend did constituted rape and she should call the police. Trini agreed that he had tried to rape her, but she did not want to call the police. Trini reasoned that if she called the police her boyfriend would indeed be arrested, but then his family would put her out. Being homeless with no place to go was a risk she was unwilling to take, even if it meant dealing with him trying to force himself on her. Trini did what the vast majority of victims in her situation do. She chose to manage the situation on her own without involving the police.

Master Manipulators

Sometimes victims do not leave their abuser because he or she is a master manipulator capable of keeping them in extremely dangerous relationships. Every abuser is a manipulator to some degree. The worst know how to use a variety of manipulative techniques to control victims for many years. Master manipulators know how to guilt-trip, play the victim, lie, seduce, exploit the victim's insecurities, threaten, and use physical violence to control the victim and keep her in the relationship. Master manipulators have a measure of psychological control over their victims, creating the perplexing dynamic in which victims know they should leave the relationship but do not.

My good friend Monica was courageous enough to share with me the details of the abusive relationship that she endured for six years from the time she was 17-years-old. For most of that time, Monica knew she no longer wanted to be with her boyfriend, Ray, but she found it extremely difficult to end their relationship. Ray's manipulative tactics of choice were guilt-tripping, seduction, financial dependence, and physical violence.

Monica grew up in New York where she met and started dating Ray. He was several years older than Monica who admittedly was very impressionable at the time. Their relationship was turbulent from the beginning. Ray was capable of being very loving and attentive toward Monica and was generous with gifts and money which made her feel very special. He brought her around his friends and family, introduced her as his girlfriend, and made her feel like part of his family, a status that she enjoyed and embraced. But he also had a way of making her feel at fault for anything bad or negative that happened in their relationship. Before long, she discovered he was extremely jealous and did not want her to form even casual relationships with other people, neither male nor female.

It was during her college years that Ray's controlling nature was on full display. After high school Monica decided to leave New York and attend college in Boston. Ray was livid. He accused her of being the reason why they would eventually break up. He accused her of thinking too much of herself because she was now a college girl. He accused her of leaving him behind, and most absurdly, he accused her of wanting to go to college in Boston so she could cheat on him. Monica tried in vain to convince him that none of those things were true, but he would not relent. In his mind he was losing control of her, so he began to guilt-trip her about her decision.

His manipulation worked. In order to allay some of his fears, Monica made the decision to return to New York every weekend in order to spend time with Ray. It was an incredible concession. Nearly every weekend for the entire four years that she was in college, Monica packed up on Fridays and returned to New York. Not because she wanted to, but because Ray demanded she come home. Those weekends were not filled with romantic gestures or relaxing evenings. They were filled with more accusations about whom she was spending time with. It was during this time that the physical abuse started. Ray was careful not to hit her in places where the bruises would be obvious. The more friends she made, the angrier and more insecure he became, which led to more frequent physical abuse and constant accusations. She desperately wanted to end the relationship, but in her mind doing so would have meant he was right about everything. By leaving him she would confirm all his insecurities about why she left town to go to college.

In a poignant statement about her college days, Monica recalled looking at pictures taken by her sorority sisters at different events and wondering why she was not in any of the pictures. Her sorority sisters responded with one word - Ray.

After college Monica returned to New York, but the relationship did not get better. It got worse. Monica remembered thinking to herself even before she left Boston that she was going to end the relationship. With college behind her, Ray would no longer be able to guilt her into staying with him. She would surely be able to break free from him once back in New York. Unfortunately, just the opposite happened. Without a job, she made the mistake of moving in with Ray and became financially dependent on him. While living together, Ray discovered that Monica had formed many friendships while in college, both male and female, and that she intended on maintaining those friendships. This enraged him. It did not matter that Ray had several girlfriends in New York as Monica would later discover.

During one particularly heated fight, Monica pulled a gun on him. According to Monica, Ray was apparently amused that she was angry enough to threaten him with a weapon. If her actions scared or intimidated him, he did not show it at all. During another fight, Monica caught another woman coming out of their home at three in the morning. This led to yet another physical confrontation, but by now Monica was fighting back. The situation had become life threatening.

It was only after Monica discovered she was pregnant that she finally found the strength to leave Ray. As she reasoned, she could not put the safety of her child at risk by continuing to be in a violent relationship. She had to get away from him for the sake of her unborn child, and during her pregnancy she left Ray for good.

One final event confirmed to Monica that she had done the right thing by leaving Ray when she did. Six months after their break up,

Ray was convicted of raping a different girlfriend and was sent to prison for 10 years. Reflecting on the conviction, Monica remarked that forcing himself on a woman was completely within Ray's character. She was not surprised about the conviction at all. She later discovered that Ray had many domestic violence convictions on his record for assaulting other women, although she had never filed a single charge against him.

It's Time To Adapt

Historically, the anti-domestic violence movement has emphasized strategies and tactics aimed at encouraging victims to leave abusers. The vast majority of the movement's focus has been on convincing victims to take action and change their own situation. Unfortunately, today's victims are no longer responding to this mandate in the way they did in years past. For a multitude of reasons, victims are either not leaving their abuser or suffering through many years of abuse before finally leaving for good. This much is certain; the abuse dynamics between victims and offenders have changed dramatically over the last decade. This regrettable reality has caused a prolonged stagnation in efforts to further reduce domestic violence.

There is a solution, however. If we want to continue to reduce domestic violence, we have to add preventative tactics that focus on offenders and compel them to abandon their abusive behaviors.

3.

Reduce Domestic Violence Further By Focusing On Offenders

Focus On Offenders

There are two things almost every survivor will tell you about breaking free from domestic violence. The first is that a victim will only leave her abuser when she makes up her mind that enough is enough. Until she gets to this point in her mind and in her heart, she will continue to stay in the relationship and continue to endure more abuse. The second is that what victims really want is for the abuser to return to being the sweet, romantic, loving person they fell in love with initially. Put simply, victims do not want to leave their relationships. They want their intimate partner to stop being abusive.

So if this is what victims really want, why has there not been more of a push to compel offenders to stop being abusive? Why do we focus all of our preventative efforts on victims rather than focusing some of our efforts on the source of the problem, offenders? Why do we expect victims to leave abusive relationships – and get upset when they do not – but have no expectation for abusers to change their behavior?

It is because we do not really believe that offenders can change; and since we do not really believe that offenders can change, we do not expect them to. Once an abuser, always an abuser is what we believe about the vast majority of domestic violence offenders. As a result, we do not invest the energy, time, or money into trying to accomplish something that we do not believe is possible. So we continue to focus all of our efforts on convincing victims to leave abusive relationships, even though there is every indication that this strategy has reached its limits.

When we come face to face with violent abusers like Walter James, Bill Lassiter and Ray, it is hard to imagine anything that we as a society could have done to keep them from being abusive.

Walter tried to kill his wife even after he was ordered to stay away from her; Bill emotionally abused and stalked his wife even during their divorce; and Ray manipulated one girlfriend for years and raped another. They epitomize the classic definition of an abuser, a man using emotional and/or physical violence to exert power and control over his intimate partner because he believes it is his right as a man to do so. Many who work in the domestic violence field will tell you without hesitation that these types of abusers are unreachable and unchangeable; that they represent a class of offender whose abusive behavior is so ingrained they cannot change; and that trying to get them to abandon their abusive behaviors would be a futile endeavor.

When domestic violence is discussed, it is usually through the lens of horrible acts of violence committed by mean and hateful people. Because these offenders intentionally choose to hurt other people, we doubt they can be persuaded to stop being abusive. It is the intentional violence to others that troubles us. Socially speaking, we tend to draw a bright red line were violence is concerned. We have zero tolerance for violent people. We believe violent offenders are predisposed to being violent and can only be reformed or changed through the penal system. This line of thinking, however, may not be true for *all* domestic violence offenders. Many offenders can be persuaded to abandon their abusive behaviors, in spite of being violent.

Drunk Driving Lessons

For all its differences from other types of offenses, domestic violence at its core is still just criminal behavior that we want to stop. When viewed simply as unwanted criminal behavior, you realize that we have successfully changed criminal behavior for other offenses. Those successes can be used as a model to change the abusive behavior of domestic violence offenders. For example, we have successfully changed criminal behavior in the areas of driving under the influence and seat belt usage; and we are beginning the task of changing criminal behavior in areas such as driving while texting and bullying. These same methods can be utilized to change the criminal behavior of domestic violence offenders.

The best example of a criminal offense where offender behavior has changed significantly is driving under the influence. There are millions of people in America who might have driven under the influence in the past but would not dare do it now, largely because of public prevention campaigns against drunk driving. The Ad Council launched its Drunk Driving Prevention campaign in 1983. It targets males 21 to 34 and includes the memorable tagline "Friends Don't Let Friends Drive Drunk." Since this time more than 68 percent of Americans have tried to prevent someone from driving after drinking. The Ad Council further reports that yearly surveys show an increase in the number of adults 21 or older who refrain from drinking and driving. The national campaign is strongly supported with prevention campaigns from state highway patrol offices, local police departments, community organizations such as Mothers Against Drunk Driving, colleges and universities, and alcohol companies.

Additionally, states strongly stiffened the criminal penalties associated with driving under the influence (DUI) to include mandatory jail time, expensive fines, and loss of driving privileges. Aside from the mandatory jail time, the cost to defend against a DUI charge can easily top $10,000 in legal fees and court costs. The loss of driving privileges disrupts one's ability to make a living or carry out routine daily duties involving driving, and offenders can expect higher insurance premiums for years upon reinstatement. The combined effect of the public prevention campaigns and increased penalties is that significantly fewer people in America drive after drinking. The number of people who will die from alcohol related traffic accidents is less than half of what it was in the 1980s.

Yet these campaigns against drinking and driving are not directed to victims of drunk driving accidents; they are directed to *potential offenders*. The ads speak directly to offenders and admonish them not to drink and drive. Likewise, as prevention campaigns for driving while texting begin to spread and the criminal penalties stiffen, it is likely that many offenders guilty of reading and sending text messages while driving will refrain from doing so in the future as a result of a campaign's admonishment.

With the success demonstrated by prevention campaigns for driving under the influence in changing offender behavior, you would think the model would have translated easily to other offenses like domestic violence; however, the violent nature of the offense stops us from using offender targeted prevention models for domestic violence. We do not believe violent people can be persuaded to stop being violent by public service announcements, slogans, and ads; and we do not believe we should have to tell people not to be violent to one another. Yet many domestic violence offenders can be persuaded to stop being abusive by prevention campaigns if the campaigns are targeted properly and the messages resonate strongly. Drunk driving prevention campaigns demonstrate that the media can play a significant role in getting offenders to change their behavior.

If we want to continue to reduce domestic violence, we should start communicating to offenders that physical violence and other abusive behaviors should never be used to resolve conflict within relationships. It may be hard to believe, but we can no longer assume that offenders know how to stop being abusive. We should inundate potential offenders with messages teaching proper conflict resolution skills and compel them to abandon any abusive behaviors. We need to regularly convey anti-domestic violence messages to offenders starting as early as the teenage years.

Interestingly enough, I have seen signs that this is beginning to happen as a natural response to continued domestic violence. I heard an offender targeted public service announcement (PSA) airing on a local radio station after a devastating domestic triple homicide rocked Memphis. The murders happened on the morning of January 19, 2012. Pashea Fisher and her boyfriend, Sedrick Clayton, got into an argument at her home. Pashea lived with her parents and her brother. She and Sedrick had a child together. It is not known if Sedrick was living at the Fisher home or just spending the night, but at around 6:00 a.m. Pashea and Sedrick got into a heated argument that turned deadly. During the argument Sedrick pulled out a gun and threatened to kill Pashea. Pashea ran into her parent's bedroom for help. Sedrick followed her and there in the bedroom he shot and killed Pashea, her father, and her mother. Sedrick then took their child and fled the home. Pashea's brother, who was awakened by the shots, witnessed the shooting but was not harmed in the attack. Hours later Sedrick turned himself in and admitted to the shootings.

The Fishers were described as a hard-working family of faith who extended their generosity and friendship to anyone they came in contact with. There was a huge outpouring of sympathy and condolences throughout the community in the wake of the tragedy, prompting at least one television station to broadcast the entire three-casket funeral live.

A local radio station, WRBO, started playing an anti-domestic violence PSA in response to the murders. The announcer spoke directly to the station's male listeners imploring them to treat their wives, girlfriends, and significant others with love and respect. There was no suggestion that women should leave abusive relationships, get help, or do anything. The focus of the PSA was solely on men, imploring them to not be abusive.

Around the same time I saw another anti-domestic violence PSA on a local cable station. The commercial featured a young black couple in their home engaged in a heated verbal argument. The commercial depicted the couple yelling vehemently at each other, then separating themselves to different rooms. The commercial then focused on the man. He took a second to calm himself and reflect. He then smiled, rejoined the woman, and engaged her in a calm discussion. The final admonition from the announcer implored men to *"Think before it's too late."*

While neither the radio PSA nor the television PSA was as impactful as the *Friends Don't Let Friends Drive Drunk* ads, the mere fact that they were produced and aired showed that other concerned groups in Memphis had come to the conclusion that more prevention efforts needed to be directed toward the source of the problem, offenders.

The Secret To Significantly Reducing Domestic Violence

It is not enough, however, to just communicate anti-abuse messages to potential offenders in a general way. If we want to significantly reduce domestic violence within a particular city or community we have to unleash the *power of a focused attack*. We have to specifically target the highest offending demographic groups with anti-abuse messages and tactics and win the domestic violence battle against these specific groups.

The benefits of doing this are threefold: First, it will likely be discovered that the top two or three offender groups are responsible for the majority of domestic violence in the community. Taking on these demographic groups gives activists the best statistical opportunity to have a substantial impact on domestic violence. Second, activists will have the ability to specifically tailor anti-abuse messages and tactics so they will resonate with targeted groups. Last, by winning the domestic violence battle against high offender groups, activists will unleash an epidemic of domestic violence reduction that will ripple across all demographic groups. In other words, if activists can win the domestic violence battle against the highest offenders, domestic violence will fall throughout the community.

This phenomenon is well documented in criminology and other social sciences. In criminology, the basic premise is that aggressively fighting small crimes can have a disproportionate and dramatic effect on reducing major crimes. The theory is that by aggressively fighting small crimes, law enforcement sends signals to the community that no crimes of any sort will be tolerated. As a result, major crimes fall because criminals see that small crimes are being forcefully fought.

The field of criminology is full of examples of the validity of this phenomenon. One of the most famous is New York Police Department's (NYPD) aggressive crackdown on subway fare beating in the early 1990s. The NYPD, faced with the task of policing a broken, blighted, and dangerous subway system, started arresting riders who jumped turnstiles or found some other way to illegally ride the subway for free. Their focus on aggressively arresting fare beaters, a minor crime, led to a dramatic and substantial decrease in major crimes occurring in the subway system.

I personally experience this phenomenon every time I drive to Germantown, Tennessee. Germantown is a small city that borders Memphis. In Germantown the speed limits are 10 miles per hour lower than in Memphis, and Germantown's police officers notoriously and aggressively ticket speeders. Their stance on speeding is so well known and their ticketing so pervasive that you always see cars ahead of you applying their breaks and slowing down well before they cross into Germantown. The ticketing has a more important purpose, however. It sends a message to the community that Germantown is a place where even minor laws will be vigorously enforced, and this helps to keep more serious crimes down. Germantown's effective focus on a small problem, speeding, helps keep major crimes in check. There are many, many examples of the successful use of this phenomenon in criminology and elsewhere.

The same principle can be used to fight domestic violence. Win the battle against the highest offenders and the message will be sent that domestic violence will not be tolerated by anyone. By effectively focusing on the top one or two offender groups, activists will cause domestic violence to decrease throughout the community.

A Blueprint To Reduce Domestic Violence

The fight against domestic violence has reached a point where we now need to apply pressure directly to the main sources of the problem. In order to do this, activists in the community have to first determine where the problems exist. Each community needs to know exactly who the offenders are, who the victims are, and the nature of the relationship between the two.

The value of this type information cannot be overstated. As mentioned earlier, it will likely be discovered that the majority of domestic violence in a particular community is being committed by the top two or three offender groups. By identifying these groups, activists can focus their efforts on the demographics creating the most problems. At the same time, a focused strike aimed at these groups will afford activists the best opportunity to achieve a significant reduction in domestic violence spreading across all demographic groups.

One of the best and most accurate ways to do this is by collecting and analyzing demographic information from recent domestic violence arrests. Domestic violence arrest records will have the race, age, and gender of the offender and likely the victim as well. This information can be captured relatively easily. Most arrest records will also have a narrative detailing the factual allegations for the arrest. The relationship between the offender and victim can be determined from this information. Once the data has been gathered in enough sufficiency, it can then be analyzed.

The results may prove surprising. It may be discovered that within a particular community the highest offenders are married, male, whites who are between the ages of 25 and 35. Or it may be discovered that the highest offenders are male, Hispanics, between the ages of 18 and 29 who are in dating relationships. The data may even reveal that most of the domestic violence occurring in the community is between family members as opposed to intimate partners.

Once the high offender groups are identified, activists can then develop targeted anti-abuse messages and tactics for these groups. The messages and tactics should be crafted in ways that resonate with the intended demographic and compel offenders to stop being abusive.

Next, by collecting and analyzing domestic violence arrest histories of offenders, activists can determine if improvements to the criminal justice process need to be made. Although arrest histories are not as accessible as demographic information, the data on whether or not offenders have been arrested or convicted in the past for domestic violence can show activists exactly where improvements need to be made in order to deter repeat arrests. By analyzing arrest histories, activists can see what percentage of offenders are first time offenders, repeat offenders, or repeat offenders with the same victim. The results will likely prove to be eye-opening. If the recidivism rate is low, this would suggest the criminal justice process is effective. Conversely, if the recidivism rate is high, this would suggest improvements need to be made. A community's criminal justice process must hold domestic violence offenders accountable for their actions; otherwise, none of the preventative tactics utilized will produce the desired results.

Focus On Offenders means determining with great specificity the highest offending groups, targeting these groups with messages and tactics that compel offenders to abandon abusive behaviors, and winning the domestic violence fight against these groups. *Focus On Offenders* also means finding ways to improve the criminal justice process, closing loopholes that offenders exploit, and reducing recidivism. By doing both of these things effectively, communities can expect to see domestic violence begin to decline. Moreover, this is what victims really want.

When we focus on offenders a number of possibilities become available to us to fight domestic violence. We should not assume that offenders cannot be persuaded to stop being abusive. Many of them can be. Outside of court ordered batter intervention programs, there has been little effort directed toward getting offenders to leave their abusive behaviors behind. This needs to change. We can steadily reduce domestic violence in the very near future by focusing more of our efforts squarely on offenders.

4.

Determining The Primary Offenders

Who's Committing Domestic Violence?

For a long while I believed that domestic violence between same sex couples in Shelby County was on the rise. For a time it seemed I was hearing petitions for orders of protection from same sex couples several times a week which was unusually high. Normally, I might only hear petitions involving same sex couples a few times per month. I reasoned that if petitions for orders of protection from same sex couples were on the rise, then domestic violence between same sex couples was probably on the rise as well. This conclusion seemed to be in line with the fact that more people in Shelby County were now identifying themselves as gay or lesbian. Maybe same sex couples were beginning to feel more comfortable availing themselves of protective services from the courts and the police, thus resulting in more petitions and arrests whenever dangerous conflict arose. All this seemed very reasonable to me, but I did not know for sure whether any of it was actually true.

I had a similar thought about women who were being arrested for domestic violence. It seemed to me more police officers were determining that the woman involved in the domestic incident was the primary aggressor. I got the sense that the number of women who were being arrested for domestic violence was on the rise. This thought was bolstered the night I was presented with an arrest warrant in which my old college roommate was the victim.

As a magistrate, it is always surreal when you are presented with a warrant that contains allegations concerning someone you know. This has happened to me on many occasions involving both family and friends. Of course ethically I cannot make any decisions on the warrants, but I hate to discover that someone close to me is either a victim or a defendant. On this particular evening, I was presented with an arrest warrant for Sabrina Ivy. I had never met Sabrina, but I knew my former college roommate and friend, Cliff Lane, was currently dating her. Sabrina had been arrested about an hour earlier, and now a request was being made to formally charge her with domestic violence stalking. Cliff was the victim.

What made the arrest even more shocking was that Cliff and I had recently discussed the problems he was having trying to end the relationship with her. He had reached out to me seeking advice on how to handle the situation. I quickly discovered why he contacted me. His relationship with Sabrina had become violent and he could not get her to leave him alone.

Cliff confided in me that the relationship had turned toxic and dangerous after only about six or seven months of dating. According to Cliff, Sabrina was prone to fits of rage whenever she got angry. Initially, Sabrina was fine with the knowledge that Cliff was also dating other women, but as time went on she grew less and less comfortable with this arrangement. Cliff was unwilling to agree to an exclusive relationship with Sabrina and this caused considerable conflict. During one heated argument Sabrina began to strike and shove Cliff. He said he did not hit her back, but he did put her in a bear hug in order to stop her from hitting him. Eventually, Sabrina calmed down and the situation de-escalated. Cliff said the incident disturbed him immensely, but he did not think it would happen again. It just confirmed for him that Sabrina was not the woman he wanted a long-term relationship with.

The violence did not stop, however; and after the second physical confrontation he wisely decided to end the relationship with Sabrina immediately. In addition to not wanting to be in a violent relationship, he feared that somehow the tables would be turned on him, and he would be the one hauled off to jail even though he was never the aggressor in any of their fights. He knew if the police were called he would be placing his fate in someone else's hands. He was not willing to take that chance. Cliff told Sabrina the relationship was over and they both needed to go their separate ways. Sabrina, however, had no interest in ending their relationship.

Cliff related to me how Sabrina would show up at his apartment, continuously bang on his door, and yell at him. At first he tried to ignore her in hopes that she would go away, but she never would.

Eventually, embarrassment would get the best of him and he would open the door and allow her to come in. Once inside the arguing would begin again. By the time Cliff contacted me he was distraught. Nothing he said to her mattered. She was not going to let the relationship end. Cliff felt she was using the fact that he was a nice guy against him. Whenever he tried to ignore her or cut off communication she would call his cell phone incessantly or cause a scene at his home in order to get him to talk to her again.

He asked me if Sabrina's behavior was egregious enough to warrant an order of protection against her. I knew then the situation had affected his ability to process what was happening to him. I told him in no uncertain terms he should call the police the next time Sabrina came to his home and refused to leave. I confirmed to him he was risking his own arrest every time they fought, and under no circumstances should he ever let her in his apartment again. To my surprise, Cliff stated to me that he was reluctant to call the police on Sabrina even though she was clearly harassing and stalking him. When I asked why, he stated he really did not want her to be arrested. He hated the idea of having to get the police involved and did not want to make trouble for her. He just wanted her to leave him alone. Unmoved by his feelings for her, I told him he should call the police the next time she showed up at his door.

Even though I knew about the problems Cliff was having, I was stunned to see a warrant for Sabrina's arrest for stalking him a few weeks later. What were the chances that another altercation would take place while I was the magistrate on duty? Not remote enough apparently.

The Affidavit of Complaint prepared by the arresting officer described events on that evening nearly identical to the pattern of stalking Cliff had described to me. While at Sabrina's home, the two got into an argument over the future of their relationship. During the argument Sabrina threatened Cliff, so he decided to return to his own home. Sabrina started sending text messages to him saying she was going to spit in his face. Sabrina then came to Cliff's apartment building where she gained entry to the roof, climbed on his second floor patio, and began pulling on the glass door. Cliff repeatedly told

Sabrina to leave his residence. She refused, at which time he called the police.

The police arrived and searched the apartment building, but were unable to locate Sabrina. While on the scene, they observed Cliff getting a text message from Sabrina saying his tires were now flat. The police and Cliff checked his vehicle and discovered that the air had indeed been let out of his tires. Still unable to locate Sabrina, the officers completed a report and left the scene. A short time later they received a second call from Cliff saying Sabrina had returned. The officers came back, and this time they were able to locate Sabrina hiding in the shadows on the first floor patio. She was placed under arrest for stalking and transported to jail.

After letting the jailers know that Sabrina's arrest warrant would have to be reviewed by a different magistrate, I immediately called Cliff to check on him. I learned the Affidavit of Complaint was not nearly as hair-raising as the actual events. According to Cliff, when it was clear to Sabrina that he was not going to let her in, she made her way to the roof of his apartment and jumped over three railings in order to gain access to his second floor patio. When Cliff saw her, she was standing on the opposite side of his sliding glass door violently pulling on the door trying to open it. He yelled to her that he was going to call the police. When she realized he was serious, she disappeared. Hours later after the police left, he heard strange noises at this same patio door. When he went to investigate, he saw Sabrina trying to pry her way in again. In a panic, he quickly called the police a second time. After a second search, the police were about to leave again when one of the officers noticed something moving in the shadows of his first floor patio. The officer drew his weapon and told Sabrina that if she was out there she had better come in. Sabrina then revealed herself, came into the apartment, and was arrested. She had to be taken into custody at gunpoint because the officers could not clearly see her on the patio. Cliff said as the police were handcuffing her she was in a rage yelling at him, "Why are you letting them do this to me?" The whole experience had shaken him to the core.

In the days that followed, I visited Cliff at his apartment. He showed me the first floor patio where Sabrina was found hiding. He pointed out to me that in order to get on his first floor patio from outside one would have to jump down onto it from the roof. It was easily a 12-foot drop. The image of Sabrina getting on the patio was startling. She had jumped down onto a small patio in the dead of night in order to escape detection. She could have broken both her legs. Cliff lived on the sixth floor of his apartment building. If she had misjudged the landing, she would have fallen to her death. If she had managed to get into his apartment, violence would have certainly erupted. I assured him that he had done the right thing by calling the police. The situation had ended the only way it could have, with someone going to jail.

Cliff's experience caused me to wonder about female offenders in Shelby County. How typical was this type of domestic violence? Nationally women perpetrated about 20 percent of all domestic violence incidents. Was the number of female offenders on the rise in Shelby County or had Sabrina Ivy biased my perception of this? The only way to know for sure would be to collect and analyze the data on Shelby County's domestic violence arrests.

Identifying The Highest Offender Groups

It is imperative that domestic violence activists in every county, city, or town determine exactly who the offenders are for their community. You have to know who the primary offenders are with great specificity so that a targeted anti-domestic violence plan can be developed. The high offender groups will be different from community to community so neither national surveys nor state-wide surveys can be relied upon to tell you who they are. Additionally, assumptions and anecdotal information about offenders, even from longtime activists in the community, may prove to be inaccurate. The only way to know for certain is to gather and analyze offender data in each community.

The most accurate way to do this is to locate and collect the charging documents for all the domestic violence arrests occurring in the community. Analyzing at least one year of this data should provide enough information to get a very accurate picture of who the primary offenders are. The charging documents usually consist of a record of arrest and a supporting narrative stating the charge and allegations. Sometimes these two records are combined into one document. In most jurisdictions the local prosecutor's office will have these files. In other jurisdictions the police department will have them.

It is important to obtain arrest records because they will contain the offender's sex, race, and age. Hopefully, they will also contain the victim's sex, race, and age. If not, the victim's demographic information may be kept separately for privacy reasons. Efforts should be made to collect demographic information on both the offender and the victim. The arrest narrative will tell you the relationship between the offender and the victim, and sometimes it will state the reason for the altercation. This is also valuable information. Once this information is located and gathered in enough sufficiency for it to be statistically reliable, it can then be entered into a spreadsheet and analyzed.

In performing this analysis for Shelby County, specifically Memphis and unincorporated Shelby County, I collected data on 829 domestic violence arrests occurring between October 2011 and October 2012. For each arrest I captured the offender's sex, race, and age; the victim's sex, race and age; the relationship between the victim and the offender; and the reason for the altercation. I then analyzed the data to determine the highest offender groups:

Highest Offender Groups

1) black, males, ages 20-29 (comprised 26% of all domestic violence arrests)
2) black, males, ages 30-39 (comprised 14% of all domestic violence arrests)
3) black, females, ages 20-29 (comprised 11% of all domestic violence arrests)

The results indicated that the highest offender group was black males from ages 20 to 29. This group accounted for 26 percent of the domestic violence arrests in Shelby County. The second highest offender group was black males from ages 30 to 39, accounting for 14 percent of the domestic violence arrests. The third highest offender group was black females from ages 20 to 29, accounting for 11 percent of the domestic violence arrests. Together these three offender groups accounted for 51 percent of all domestic violence arrests. They represented the most problematic sources of domestic violence in Shelby County. If activists in Shelby County were to focus their preventative efforts on these three demographics, they would be attacking the offender groups who were responsible for over half the domestic violence arrests in the county.

The data also gives activists an overall snapshot of the domestic violence problem in the community. In Shelby County, 73 percent of the offenders were male; 83 percent of the offenders were black; 49 percent of the offenders were under the age of 30; and 62 percent of the offenders were in a boyfriend/girlfriend relationship with the victim.

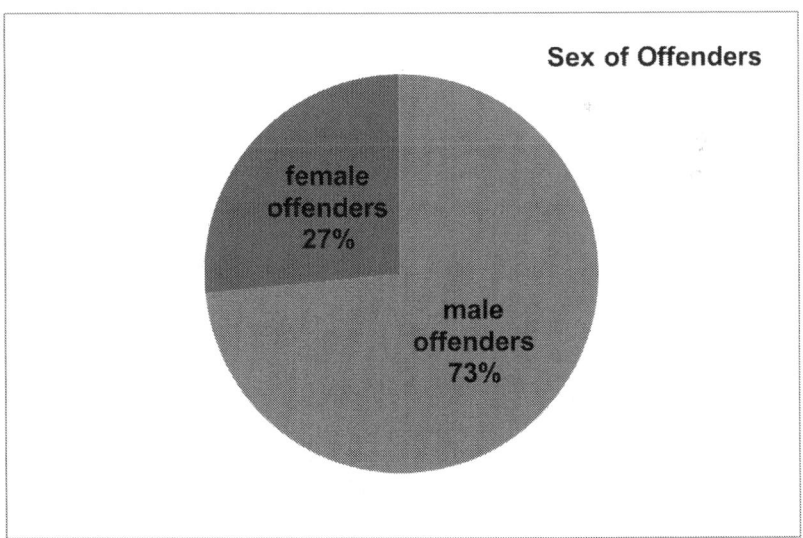

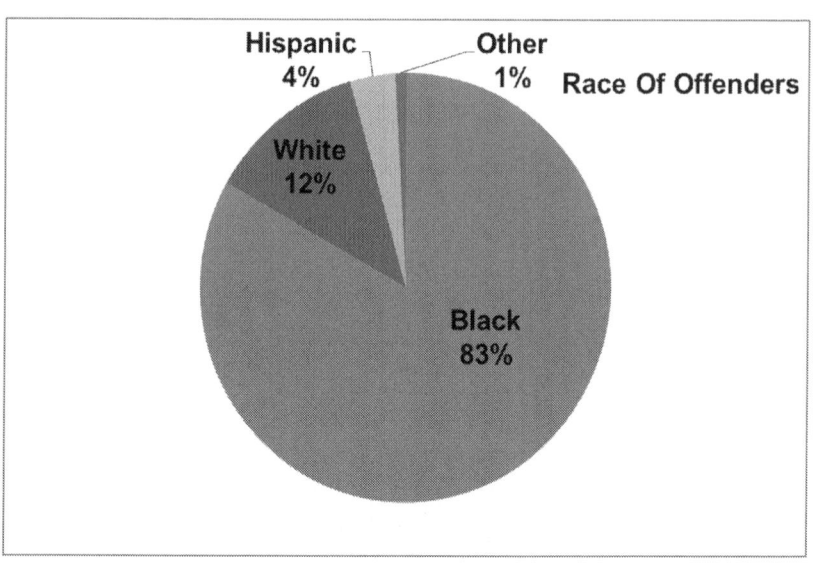

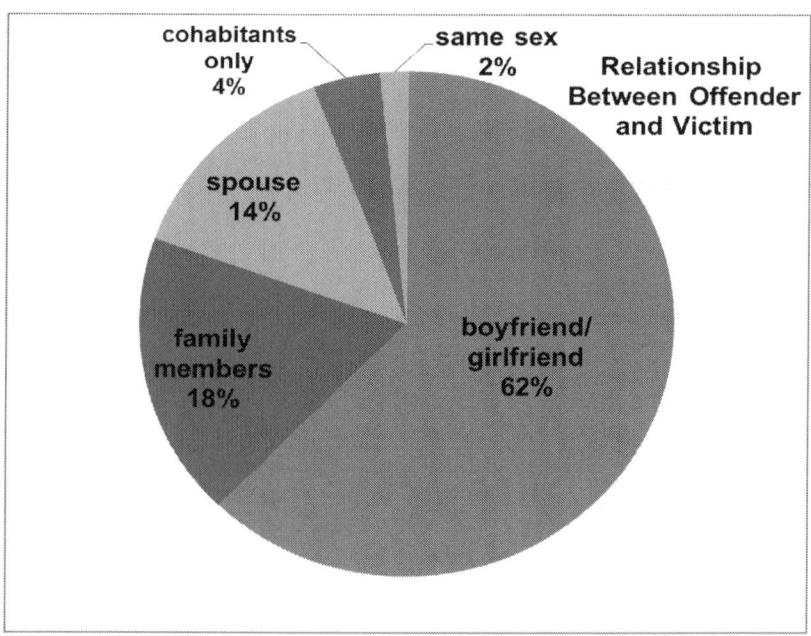

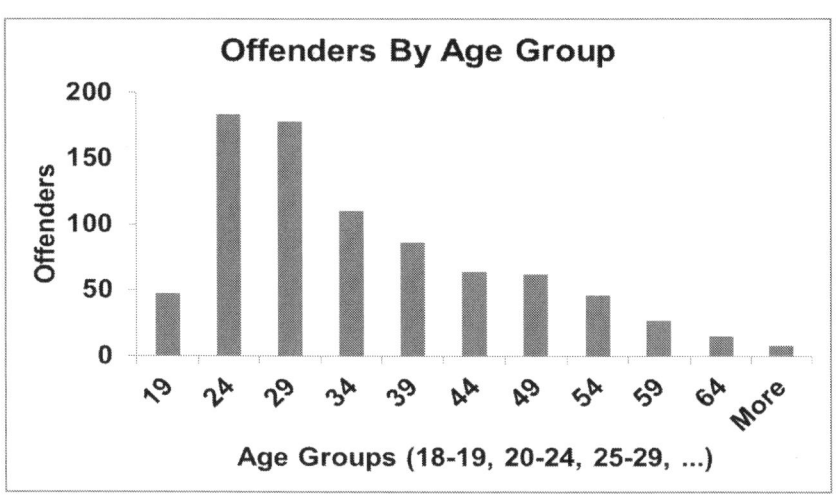

Revealing Age Data

When the data is analyzed some of the results will confirm what is already suspected about who the offenders are in the community. Other results may reveal some surprising and useful information about offenders.

For Shelby County the demographic results on sex and race were largely expected, but the age distribution of offenders was very surprising. What was immediately apparent was the high number of offenders in the 20 to 29 age range. This 10-year age period accounted for an astounding 44 percent of all domestic violence arrests. The data analysis showed overwhelmingly that this was the age range activists in Shelby County needed to concentrate on in order to further reduce domestic violence. Offenders in this age range were so prone to arrest for domestic violence that female offenders in this age range were the third highest offending group, even though females only accounted for 27 percent of all arrests. Fifty-two percent of female offenders were ages 20 to 29.

This analysis revealed that 20-year-olds had a very high propensity to resolve domestic conflict with violence or abuse. When arrests for 18 and 19-year-olds were included, the results showed that half of the adult domestic violence offenders in Shelby County were under the age of 30.

Additionally, the data revealed the next problematic age range was 30 to 39. This age range accounted for 24 percent of all domestic violence arrests.

The value of the information revealed by the age analysis cannot be overstated. Activists in Shelby County could now take on the primary age groups responsible for the largest portions of domestic violence, giving them the best opportunity to make significant strides. They could now zero in on the causes of domestic violence for young adults in the community and develop targeted anti-abuse campaigns for this particular demographic. For example, activists could choose to engage 20-year-olds with presentations at vocational schools and colleges, workshops at their places of worship, or media campaigns on social internet sites. Additionally, they might decide to engage them with targeted PSAs on TV or radio.

Corroborating Relationship Data

The relationship data for Shelby County provided unexpected and interesting results as well. The purpose of collecting this information was to determine which domestic relationships were yielding the most domestic violence. The results proved to be just as revealing as the age distribution.

Violence or abuse in Shelby County is considered to be *domestic* if certain relationships between the offender and the victim exist. If the offender and victim are or were intimate partners they have a domestic relationship; if the offender and victim are or were family members related by blood or marriage they have a domestic relationship; and if the offender and victim live or once lived together, they are considered to have a domestic relationship. In capturing the relationship data, intimate partners were divided into three groups: former or current spouse, former or current boyfriend or girlfriend, and former or current same sex partner. *Family Members* remained its own category, and *Cohabitants Only* remained its own category.

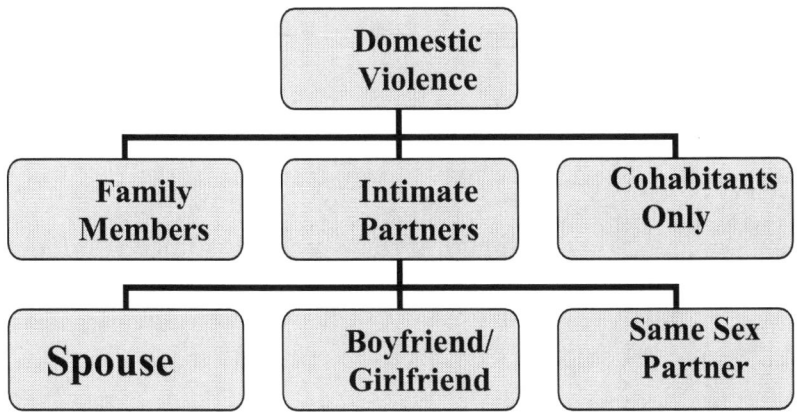

For me it was completely unexpected that boyfriend/girlfriend relationships would comprise an unbelievable 62 percent of arrests. This category produced the most arrests by an overwhelming amount. What was it about the nature of boyfriends and girlfriends that caused this type of relationship to produce more domestic violence arrests than any other type of relationship? When viewed in a vacuum the answer was not clear, but when viewed in relation to the age data the answer became apparent.

Boyfriend/girlfriend relationships produced the most domestic violence arrests because young adults tended to be in this type of intimate relationship more than any other. Seventy-three percent of offenders ages 20 to 29 indicated they were the boyfriend or girlfriend of the victim. Sixty-one percent of offenders ages 30 to 39 indicated they were the boyfriend or girlfriend of the victim. When examined in connection with the age data, it made sense that the vast majority of offenders would be the boyfriend or girlfriend of the victim because half of all offenders were under the age of 30. Youth tended to be a strong contributing factor of domestic violence in Shelby County and the relationship data bolstered this conclusion. If activists wanted to key in on this information and target potential offenders based on boyfriend/girlfriend dating habits, they could develop anti-abuse ads to be displayed in movie theaters, restaurants, or dance clubs.

Another surprising result revealed itself in the relationship data. Arrests for domestic violence between family members were higher than arrests involving spouses. Family member domestic violence accounted for 18 percent of arrests, while spousal domestic violence accounted for 14 percent of arrests. The traditional perception that abusive husbands were the main offenders of domestic violence did not prove to be true in Shelby County. In fact, if activists in Shelby County were only employing preventative tactics aimed at protecting victims from their abusive husbands, they would be missing the boat entirely. In 80 percent of the arrests the relationship between the offender and the victim was either boyfriend/girlfriend or family members.

Again, the usefulness of each community collecting and analyzing this type of data cannot be overemphasized. The clarity and depth that the results provide in determining who the offenders are is powerful. For example, activists in Shelby County now knew from a quantitative standpoint to focus their attention on young, black adults in dating relationships in order to have the greatest impact on reducing domestic violence. By examining the data, activists in other communities can make similar determinations and discover exactly which demographics and relationships require the most immediate attention.

Victim Data Matched Offender Data

If the arrest records contain victim information, activists in the community can also see who the victims are. In Shelby County the demographic data on victims closely matched the demographic data of offenders. Victims tended to be of the opposite sex, the same race, and in the same age range as offenders. Seventy-five percent of victims were female and 82 percent of victims were black. Similar to the age distribution for offenders, 50 percent of victims were under the age of 30.

The two demographic groups that accounted for the largest number of victims were black females ages 20 to 29 and black females ages 30 to 39. These two groups accounted for 28 percent and 15 percent of victims, respectively.

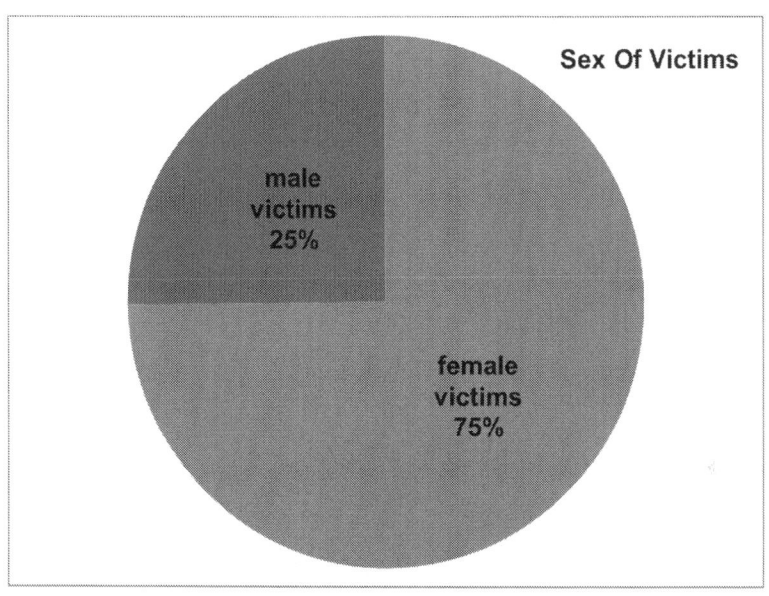

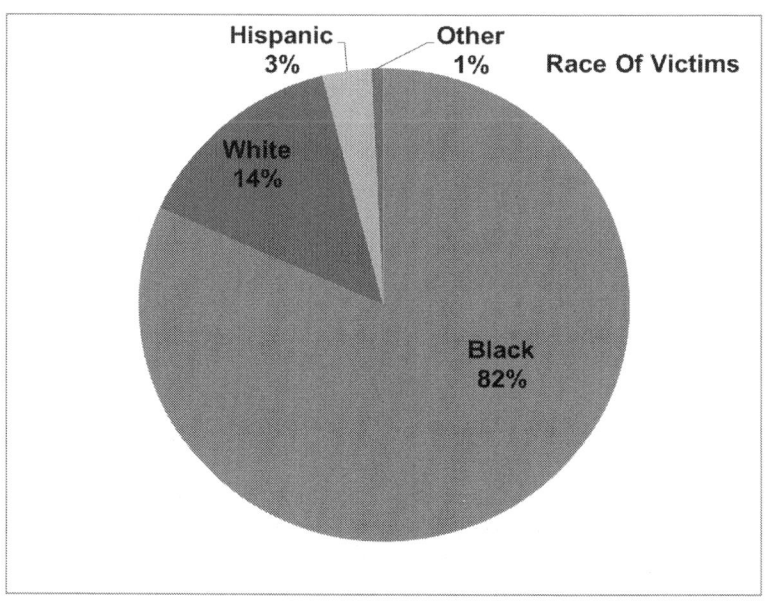

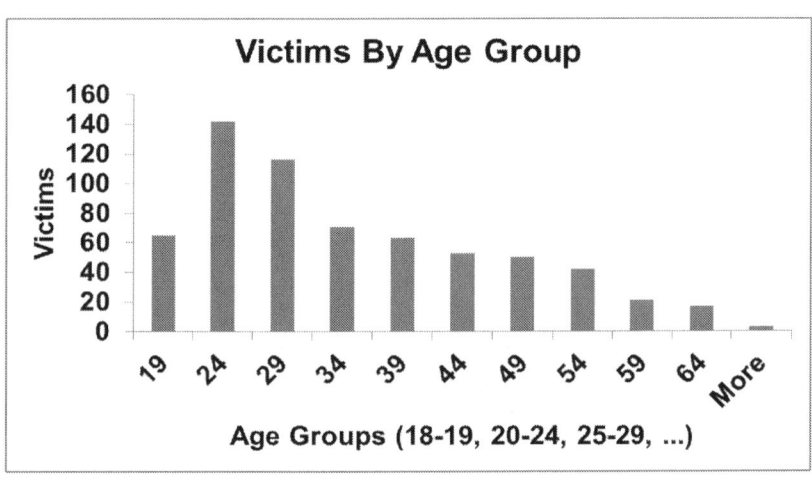

Intimate Partner Violence

Some activists are now starting to narrow their domestic violence focus to only include intimate partner violence. These activists are more interested in abuses occurring within these relationships. Violence occurring between family members and those who are only cohabitants often fall outside the general power and control model that activists are trained to identify and combat. In light of this, I thought it appropriate to demonstrate how to obtain intimate partner statistics once the data has been collected.

In order to find trends in intimate partner violence the relationship between the offender and the victim must be known. The relationship must either be past or present boyfriend/girlfriend, past or present spouse, or past or present same sex partner. Just knowing the sex of the offender and the victim is not enough. For example, if a brother gets arrested for assaulting his sister, this would not be intimate partner violence because the offender and victim are family members. An intimate relationship must exist. If the relationship data can be collected, communities can easily determine how much intimate partner violence is occurring and who the primary offenders are.

In May 2002, the DOJ conducted an intimate partner domestic violence survey. The agency profiled 3,750 intimate partner domestic violence cases filed that month in 16 large urban counties, including Shelby County. The DOJ found that 84 percent of the cases involved a male defendant and a female victim; 12 percent of the cases involved a female defendant and a male victim; and 4 percent of the cases involved same sex offenders and victims.

Would Shelby County's current intimate partner violence statistics be the same as the DOJ's findings after 10 years, or had there been a shift in who was perpetrating this type of violence? An analysis of Shelby County's intimate partner statistics yielded the following results:

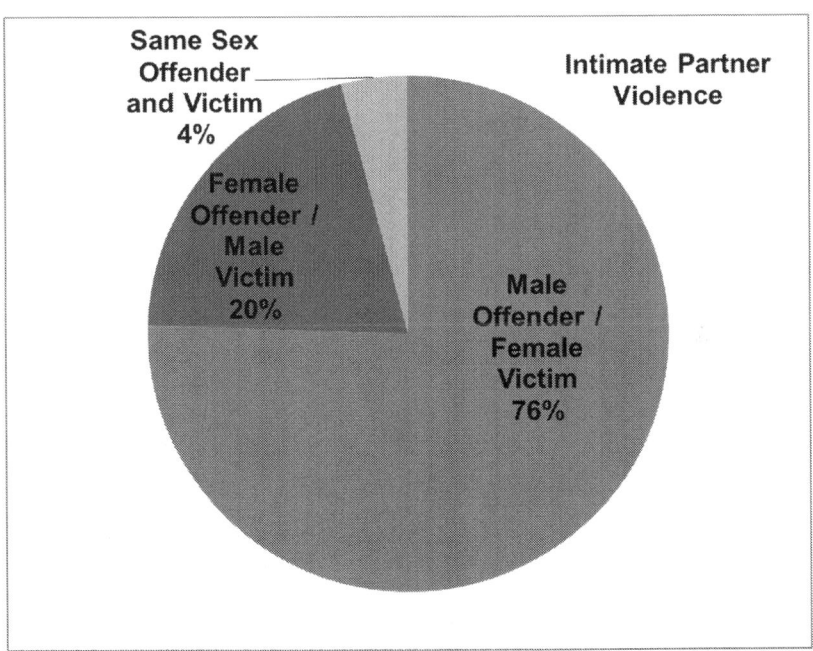

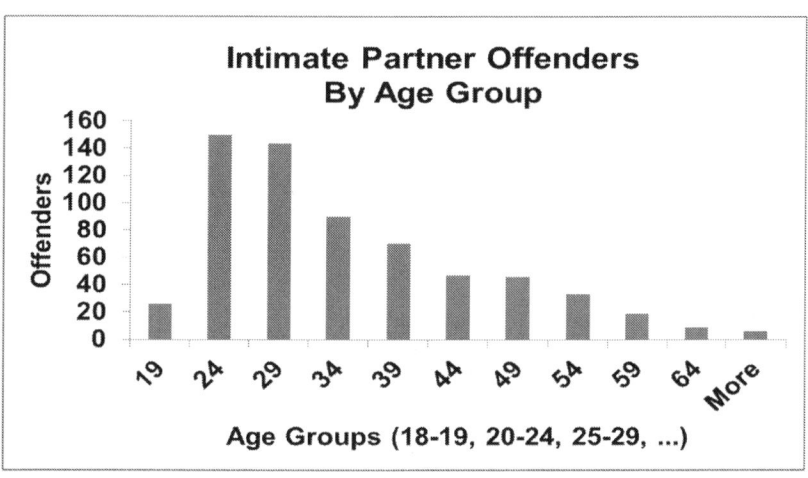

The results of the intimate partner analysis tended to confirm what I had perceived about female offenders. There had been a noticeable increase in the percentage of females being arrested for intimate partner domestic violence. Female intimate partner offenders accounted for 20 percent of arrests in Shelby County as compared to 12 percent of arrests in the DOJ's study. Of course, the DOJ's results were compiled from 16 urban counties, so it is not quite an apples-to-apples comparison; but the study is a useful benchmark for gauging the direction of trends in intimate partner violence. Shelby County's data suggested that a higher percentage of women were being arrested for resorting to physical violence to resolve conflict within intimate relationships.

With regard to same sex offenders and victims, Shelby County's data showed no change from the DOJ's finding in 2002.

Yet again, the age distribution for intimate partner arrests showed that the most problematic age range was 20 to 29. This age range accounted for 46 percent of the arrests for intimate partner domestic violence.

Family Domestic Violence

Seven twenty-two Lester Street was the scene of the most shocking mass murders in Memphis' history. The media dubbed the killings the *Lester Street Massacre,* and it was a fitting description for the horrific acts that took place in the early morning hours of March 2, 2008.

On March 3, 2008, police arrived at 722 Lester Street to find four adults murdered, two children murdered, and three more children critically wounded. The adults were Cecil Dotson, his girlfriend Marissa Williams, and their two friends, Hollis Seals and Shindri Roberson. They had been shot multiple times with a semi-automatic handgun. The children, all five of whom belonged to Cecil Dotson, were between the ages of nine years and two months and had been stabbed with a knife or bludgeoned. Three of those children managed to survive the attack. The most miraculous survivor was 9-year-old Cecil "CJ" Dotson, Jr. who was found in a bathtub some 40 hours after the attack with a 4 ½-inch knife protruding from his skull.

Initial theories about the murders were that they were gang-related and involved more than one perpetrator. The thinking was that with so many people dead, including four adults, this had to be the work of multiple individuals. No one person would be able to kill four adults at one time. If the attacker were a lone assailant, someone should have been able to get away or subdue the attacker while his attention was on other people. Additionally, there were no apparent signs of a break-in or robbery, leading investigators to believe that the victims knew the perpetrators and had allowed them into the home. Once inside, the perpetrators killed or attempted to kill Cecil Dotson and everyone in his home that night.

This theory, however, was quickly dispelled in shocking detail by the eldest of the three survivors. CJ told investigators that the lone attacker was his uncle, Jesse Dotson. CJ told investigators that when the shooting started he ran to call the police, but had to fight off his uncle before ending up in the bathtub with a kitchen knife embedded in his head. When the paramedics found CJ the next day, they thought he was dead until he started twitching. According to CJ, Uncle Jesse was the one who had killed his father, mother, their friends, and his siblings.

It was later revealed that the gruesome murders were the result of an argument between the brothers, Cecil and Jesse. During the argument Jesse pulled out a gun and shot Cecil. He then slaughtered everyone else in the house, including the children, in attempt to cover up Cecil's murder. He left the scene riding one of the children's bikes thinking that everyone was dead. To Jesse Dotson's surprise, CJ, his 5-year-old brother, and his 2-month-old sister survived. Jesse Dotson, who eventually confessed, received six death penalty sentences for each of the murders, plus an additional 120 years in jail for each of the attempted murders.

Family Domestic Violence Is A Big Problem

It is worth noting again that in Shelby County domestic violence involving family members was the second largest category of domestic violence, even more prevalent than spousal abuse. The high percentage of family member violence, however, comes as no surprise to those of us who work in the domestic violence field. Conflicts between people related by blood or marriage frequently erupt in to violence and arrests. Moreover, no family relationship seems to be more prone to violence than another. Those arrested for family domestic violence include mothers, fathers, brothers, sisters, uncles, aunts, grandparents, and in-laws of victims.

As more communities analyze their domestic violence data, it will likely be found that violence between family members is more widespread and more problematic than originally thought. In fact, it will likely be discovered that the failure to address domestic violence between family members means not combating a large portion of domestic violence within the community. Shelby County's family domestic violence data revealed the following:

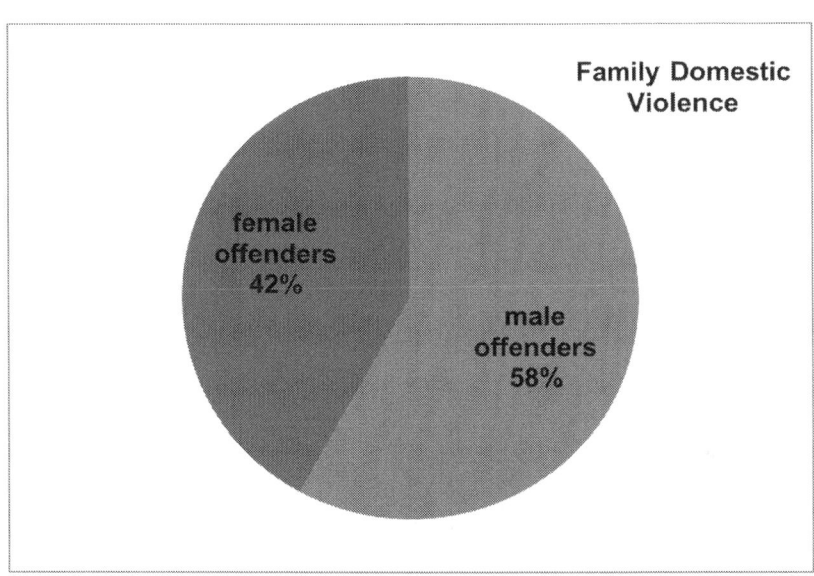

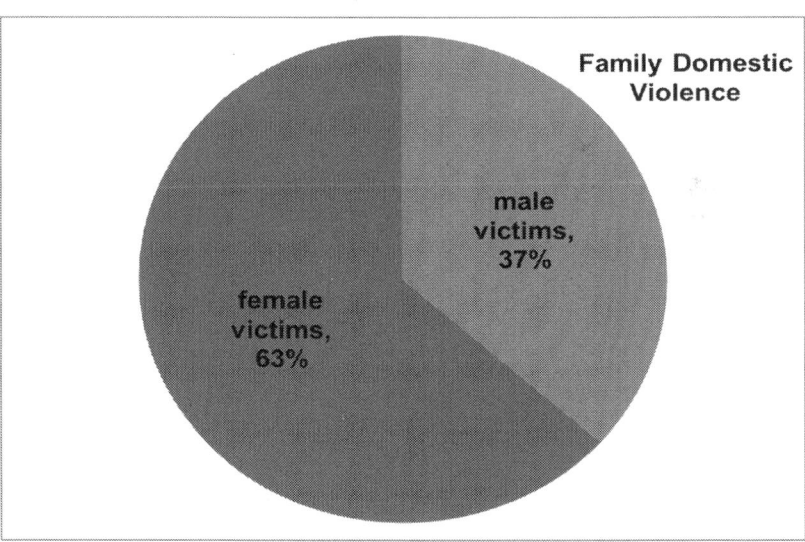

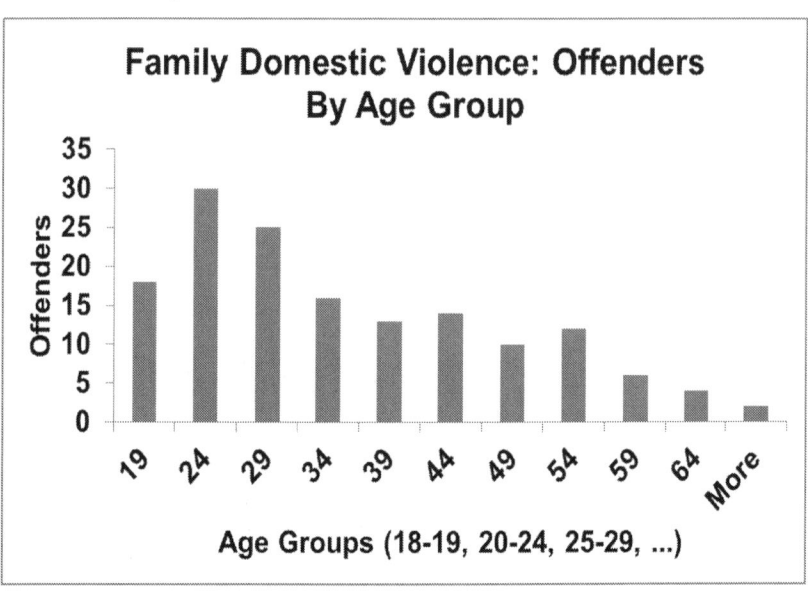

The root causes of family violence differ greatly from the causes of intimate partner violence. The vast majority of intimate partner violence originates from the offender trying to exert power and control over the actions of the victim in an abusive manner. The causes of family violence are varied, ranging from disputes over money, personal property, and drug addiction, to disputes that are the result of years of tension between family members. As a result, combating family violence is challenging.

What the data revealed about domestic violence between family members in Shelby County is that both sexes strongly perpetrated violence against both sexes. Male offenders were violent toward both male and female family members, and female offenders were violent toward both male and female family members as well. Male offenders accounted for 6 out of every 10 arrests.

Amazingly, even though the offenders and victims were more evenly distributed based on gender, when it came to age the same problematic demographic, ages 20 to 29, was found to be the highest offending group. In fact, over 49 percent of the offenders arrested for domestic violence involving a family member were under the age of

30. This was an unexpected result. It was expected that domestic violence involving family members would have a fairly even distribution across all age ranges since conflicts were observed indiscriminately in all types of family relationships. The finding that 20 to 29 year olds were the highest offenders of family member violence just like they were the highest offenders of intimate partner violence was surprising.

If there was any doubt that youth was a strong contributing factor to domestic violence in Shelby County, the results of the family member violence analysis extinguished that doubt. The age range of 20 to 29 had been found to be the highest offending demographic in three different analyses; overall domestic violence, intimate partner domestic violence, and family member domestic violence. Clearly this age range represented ground zero in the fight to reduce domestic violence in Shelby County.

Limitations Of Arrest Data

For all its usefulness in identifying high offender groups, this type of data analysis has limitations that activists should be aware of. If the data is collected in the way I suggest, it will only reflect adult domestic violence activity. This is because in most communities juvenile offenders are handled separately from adult offenders and their records are generally entitled to a very high degree of privacy, making access to them extremely difficult. Thus, the data will be limited to information on adult offenders starting at age 18.

Additionally, if any biases exist in the police department's arrest procedure it will be reflected in the data. For example, if female offenders are generally given an opportunity to leave the scene of a domestic incident in order to cool off, but male offenders are not given that option, this bias will be reflected in the data; or if one race of offenders is systematically treated differently than another race of offenders when it comes to arrests, this disparate treatment will be reflected in the data.

Finally, activists may find they do not have as much data on victims as they do on offenders. Victim information can be spotty either because police officers do not collect it with as much diligence as they do the offender information or because it is subject to a higher degree of privacy than offender information and is therefore not readily available. Activists should push hard to obtain as much victim information as possible. The insight that it provides in terms of showing a clear picture of the local domestic violence problem is essential.

5.

Targeting High Offenders

Crafting The Message

Once activists know who to target with prevention efforts, the question becomes what to say to them? What message or admonishment should be imparted that will compel offenders to abandon their abusive behaviors? It is a tough question and the answer is not obvious. After the Fisher murders in Memphis, local radio station WRBO aired a PSA encouraging men to treat their intimate partners with love and respect. Was this the right message? Did it resonate with offenders who heard it and persuade them to stop being abusive? The domestic violence PSA that I saw on a local cable channel told men to *"Think before it's too late."* Did this message leave an impression on the offenders who saw it?

To help answer this question for Shelby County I tracked one other piece of information that I hoped would shed some light on how to craft the prevention message. For 151 arrests I noted the *reason for the altercation* as stated in the Affidavit of Complaint. My goal was to see what abusers and victims were fighting about. Police officers are not required to put the reason for the altercation in the arrest report, and most of the time they do not; but when the reason was included, I captured that information and counted how many times it was given. Below are the results for arrests involving intimate partners:

Reason for the Altercation

1) *Cheating or inappropriate contact with the opposite sex (given in 29% of arrests)*
2) *Abuser or victim feeling disrespected (given in 13% of arrests)*
3) *Abuser harassing or stalking the victim (given in 10% of arrests)*
4) *Dispute over personal property (given in 9% of arrests)*
5) *Ending the relationship (given in 9% of arrests)*
6) *Trying to put the abuser out of the home (given in 9% of arrests)*
7) *Dispute over the children (given in 7% of arrests)*

8) *Violation of an order of protection or stay-away order (given in 5% of arrests)*
9) *Dispute over money (given in 4% of arrests)*
10) *Trying to control the victim's actions (given in 3% of arrests)*
11) *Dispute over the use of drugs or alcohol (given in 2% of arrests)*

Victims of domestic violence will not be surprised by the results of this analysis. The most common reason given was allegations of cheating or inappropriate contact with the opposite sex. This reason was given 29 percent of the time when the cause of the altercation was included in the arrest record. Victims often related to officers that the abuser accused them of cheating; but this reason also included altercations that happened because the abuser or victim discovered text messages or phone calls from someone of the opposite sex. In fact, inappropriate contact with someone of the opposite sex actually resulted in more domestic violence arrests than allegations of outright cheating.

Altercations arising from the victim or abuser feeling disrespected produced the next largest amount of domestic violence arrests at 13 percent. This reason manifested itself in a number of different ways, but the common strand was that violence erupted because one intimate partner said or did something that offended the other. After this reason, the next four were given in nearly equal amounts.

Tracking the reasons for altercations is useful because it helps shape anti-abuse messages. Activists need to craft prevention messages that tell offenders to stop being abusive and provide a proper conflict resolution skill that can be used in situations where the risk for violence is high. These messages need to be within the context of real situations that often result in domestic violence, like cheating. When this is done effectively, there is more of a chance that offenders who are exposed to the messages will choose to resolve conflicts in a non-abusive way.

Targeted Messages And Tactics

I visited the YouTube website and watched some of the most viewed anti-domestic violence PSAs. The most viewed PSA depicts the harsh brutality of domestic violence and implicitly suggests that victims have to leave abusers. The PSA shows a young white woman covered in bruises on her face and neck staring directly into the camera as if it is a mirror. At the beginning of the PSA she has two black eyes, a large laceration on her forehead, and bruising around her neck. As she touches one black eye and the laceration on her head, those injuries disappear; but then, just as those injuries disappear, other past injuries to her face begin to appear. An even larger and more pronounced contusion appears on the other side of her forehead, her other eye turns even blacker, and blood starts to run from her nose revealing that it is has been broken in the past. The PSA invokes sadness, anger, and fear for the victim, particularly as she reacts in terror to the possible presence of the abuser in the closing seconds. The message displayed at the end of PSA says, "It Rarely Stops." The goal of the PSA is to drive home the message to victims that offenders will not stop being abusive.

The next most viewed PSA depicts a middle-age white man at a restaurant table with his two small children. The waitress comes over, begins to pour coffee into his cup and spills it on the table. At this point the man gets very angry and starts using profanity about the waitress spilling his coffee. The children apprehensively look away from their father as if they know what is about to happen. The father angrily tells the waitress that she spilled his coffee. She apologizes, but then the father jumps up, grabs her by the throat, and slams her down on another table. He calls her a bitch as he snatches the coffee pot from her and pours it all over her face. The waitress screams loudly as she is attacked, but no one in the restaurant comes to her rescue. Finally, the man smacks her to the floor and returns to his seat with his children. The announcer then says, "You wouldn't get away with it here. You shouldn't get away with it at home." The goal of this PSA is to emphasize how wrong domestic violence is by showing what it would like if inflicted upon a stranger in public.

Both PSAs are professionally produced and their prevention messages are unambiguous and forceful. The question is, are they effective in preventing domestic violence? Does the first PSA effectively persuade victims to leave abusers? Does the second PSA provoke offenders to stop being abusive? The answer, of course, is maybe. It is hard to say whether the PSAs are effective without rigorously testing them on the target audience; but it is safe to say their effectiveness likely increases among victims and offenders who share similar demographic traits with the main characters.

As discussed earlier, I tend to believe that victims today are very reluctant to leave abusers and do not respond strongly to this directive; but to the extent that some victims can be persuaded to leave their abuser, the first PSA would work best in communities where victims tend to be young white females.

The second PSA is directed to offenders and poignantly shows how disgusting and mean abusers are. The PSA attempts to compel offenders to stop being abusive by pointing out that they would not dare treat a stranger in the same violent way they treat their intimate partner. The underlying moral condemnation in the message is a strong tool in getting offenders to abandon abuse. This PSA would work best in communities where offenders tend to be middle-age white men.

It is not likely that either of these PSAs would be effective in Shelby County. Since Shelby County's offenders tend to be young black men, a PSA directed to this demographic would be most effective. An effective PSA would also take into consideration the reasons for altercations in Shelby County and depict a scenario that typically causes violence.

This is why I like the *Think Before It's Too Late* PSA for Shelby County. The PSA was targeted to offenders. It showed a young black couple getting into a heated argument in their home. It showed the man removing himself from the argument by going into another room for a moment, ostensibly to think about how to properly handle the dispute. It then showed the man rejoin the female and engage her in a calm, non-confrontational discussion. The PSA's scenario is realistic, not over the top, and teaches offenders how to use a non-abusive technique to handle heated arguments. Finally, the tag line reminds offenders that there are dire consequences for domestic violence. I think this PSA works well for Shelby County.

Unfortunately, I only saw it on TV once. I would have been elated to discover that the PSA was airing regularly in Shelby County, because these types of messages have to be delivered continuously in order to be effective; but I never saw it again. Offenders should be exposed to anti-abuse messages frequently and regularly. Their usage should be ubiquitous in the community. Think about how many times you see or hear a PSA or ad admonishing against drinking and driving. Now think about how many times you see or hear a PSA or ad admonishing against domestic abuse. If PSAs like *Think Before It's Too Late* were utilized regularly and the criminal justice system held offenders accountable, I believe domestic violence in Shelby County would decline substantially.

Walk Out On Domestic Violence

"Walk Out On Domestic Violence" is the tag line and central message that I would deliver to offenders if I were creating an anti-domestic violence PSA or campaign. I like this message for offenders because it accomplishes three essential goals: First, it is easy to remember and can be quickly recalled during times when potentially violent situations arise. Second, it provides a simple and easy to understand instruction that offenders can use to avoid or de-escalate potentially violent situations. The act of walking away is an effective tool for preventing domestic violence. Safety increases dramatically when offenders separate themselves from victims until cooler heads prevail. Last, the message embodies an overall societal position that domestic violence is wrong. When you walk out on something, you turn your back on it as a gesture of intolerance. Ultimately, what any PSA or campaign should endeavor to achieve is a moral shift in offenders that will cause them to abandon their abusive behaviors. Once this happens, you have successfully eliminated domestic violence in the life of the offender.

Developing effective tactics to fight domestic violence is not a one-size-fits-all proposition. Activists in each community will need to determine exactly who the high offenders are in order to develop targeted anti-abuse messages and tactics that will reverberate. PSAs are not the only tactic that should be considered. Activists should consider engaging high offenders in as many ways as possible. Many offenders will abandon their abusive behaviors when shown how to resolve disputes without resorting to violence or abuse.

6.

Teen Dating Violence

Face To Face With Teen Dating Violence

When juveniles request orders of protection against other juveniles their parents have to come to court as well. A juvenile petitioner must get a parent to file for an order of protection on his or her behalf, and the petition must be served on the parent of a juvenile respondent. On the day of the hearing, the juvenile petitioner along with his or her parent present their case as to why they need an order of protection against the juvenile respondent who has appeared with his or her parent.

The reasons that parents request orders of protection on behalf of their children vary widely. Some parents want the juveniles to stop having sex and have thus far been unsuccessful at keeping them apart. These parents are hoping that an order of protection will keep the teens separated. Some parents want the juveniles to stay away from each other because of ongoing fights between the two that have now boiled out of control. Still other parents are trying to stop one child from bullying the other.

Occasionally, juveniles will appear with their parents alleging classic domestic violence allegations. All allegations of domestic violence are serious, but there is a heightened sense of concern when the victim and the offender are teenagers. The first petition for an order of protection that I had involving domestic violence between two juveniles illustrated just how explosive these situations can be.

Janice and her mother appeared before me requesting an order of protection against her boyfriend Michael who appeared with his mother. Interestingly enough, both parents were in agreement that an order of protection needed to be issued in order to keep their children away from each other. The entire hearing might have only lasted five minutes if both parties had agreed to the order of protection, but when I asked Janice if she wanted an order of protection against Michael she said, "No." Clearly, the parents had a different view of the situation than the children. I decided to take testimony and find out what the problem was between the teenagers.

Janice and Michael were girlfriend and boyfriend and they had an infant child together. Both were 16 and both were rising seniors. It was summer, and Janice had spent the night at Michael's home so they both could spend time with their child together. On the morning of the incident, Michael's mother left for work leaving Janice, Michael, and their child at home. According to Janice, at some point during the morning Michael started receiving text messages from another girl. Michael refused to tell her who sent the text messages, causing Janice to become infuriated. A heated verbal argument ensued. It was unclear to me who struck whom first, but the two began pushing, shoving, and wrestling with each other all around the house.

Michael stated that Janice would not calm down and was in a rage for over an hour. He called his mother on his cell phone to see if she could get Janice to calm down and stop fighting. Michael's mother said she could hear Janice cussing and screaming in the background, but she could not stop working to have a conversation with her. She immediately called her sister and asked her to go to the house and see what was going on because Janice and Michael were fighting again.

When the sister arrived she could hear the two yelling and fighting in the home. She banged on the door for five minutes, but no one came to the door. Finally she decided to call the police. After she called the police, but before they arrived, Michael opened the door. He was covered in his own blood but did not appear to notice that he had been cut. The sister went in the house to find Janice holding her baby and still wielding a bloody kitchen knife. Michael had been cut across the shoulder and was bleeding profusely.

I pressed Janice to find out why she had cut Michael. She said she did not remember at what point during the argument she armed herself with the knife. She remembered that Michael was holding her down and she was trying to get up but could not. She also could not remember when she picked up her child but admitted she was holding her when she lunged at Michael, cutting him with the knife. She had missed his jugular vein by two or three inches. Janice was arrested and taken to juvenile court. Both parents testified that Janice and Michael fought regularly after Janice became pregnant and that both needed a break from each other. But Michael and Janice wanted the adults to stay out of their relationship. Michael could have easily been killed, but getting him to tell me his version of events was like pulling teeth. Though he clearly wanted the freedom to date other girls, he did not want me to order him to stay away from Janice because that meant not being able to see his child. Neither Janice nor Michael had anything to say about placing the child in danger while they were fighting with a deadly weapon.

Of course, I agreed with the parents and applauded them for doing whatever was necessary to separate Janice and Michael. It was clear that the stresses and responsibilities that came along with having a child were too much for them to handle. I could not grant Janice and her mother a permanent order of protection against Michael because the testimony tended to show that Janice was the actual aggressor; but I did agree that a brief separation was warranted. I extended the temporary order of protection through the rest of the summer and encouraged the parents to use the time to talk to their children and teach them how to resolve conflict within the relationship without resorting to violence. With any hope, they were successful in doing so.

Teen dating violence continues to be a very serious issue throughout the country. The Centers for Disease Control and Prevention surveyed high school students and found that nearly 10 percent had been assaulted by their boyfriend or girlfriend in the 12 months prior to the survey. Parents should not wait until they see signs of domestic violence to address the issue. All parents with teens need to talk to their children about teen dating violence as soon as they start dating. The conversation should not only be about what to do if he or she is assaulted, but also about not resorting to violence when inevitable conflicts arise within the relationship.

7.

Reducing Recidivism

Tracking Recidivism

If developing targeted preventative tactics aimed at reducing domestic violence among high risk offenders is the first line of attack, then implementing effective punitive deterrents for offenders is the next offensive. Doing both of these at the same time will reduce domestic violence substantially. The ideal state of affairs would be a punitive system that yielded no repeat offenders at all. In other words, every person arrested for domestic violence would be a first time offender who would never come back through the system as a repeat offender. Obviously, a recidivism rate of zero is wishful thinking, but this should be the ultimate goal of all prosecutors and courts handling domestic violence cases. If local activists have the ability to track recidivism among domestic violence offenders, I strongly urge them to do so. The results will show the effectiveness of their criminal justice system and highlight where improvements need to be made in order to further reduce recidivism.

Tracking recidivism among offenders is a little harder than tracking the demographics of offenders because arrest history information is not always readily available. As stated earlier, the race, gender, and age of the offender and usually the victim will be indicated in arrest documents that are easily obtainable from the police department or the prosecutor's office. Arrest histories of offenders may not be included with those documents, so it may take a special effort to obtain them for purposes of tracking recidivism. Additionally, a large sample of arrest histories must be collected and recorded in order for the statistical analysis to be reliable. If this information can be obtained, the results can be used to help reduce repeat domestic violence in the community.

As an example of how useful arrest history information can be, I tracked the arrest histories of offenders for 829 arrests occurring between October 2011 and October 2012 in Shelby County. I categorized each arrest into one of four categories: first domestic violence arrest; at least one prior domestic violence arrest, but no convictions; at least one prior domestic violence conviction; and at least one prior domestic violence conviction with the same victim as the current arrest. The analysis yielded the following results:

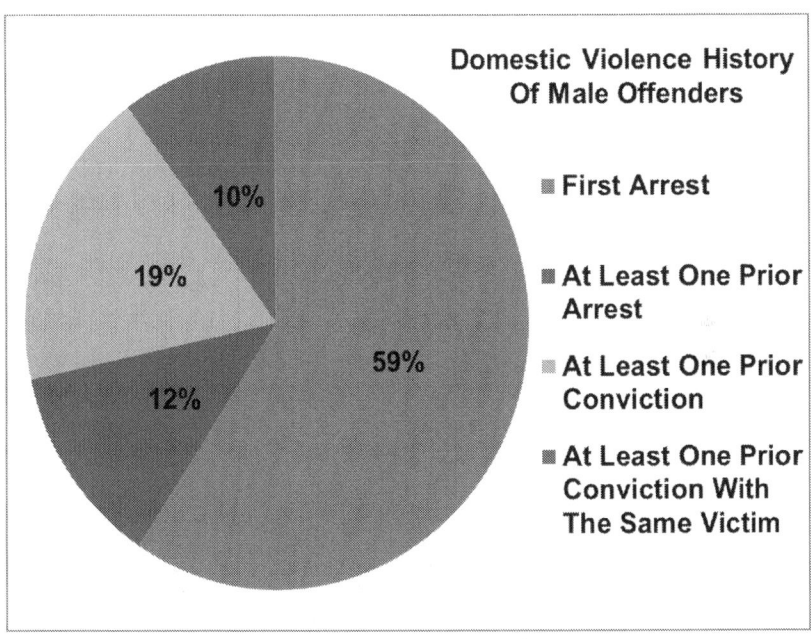

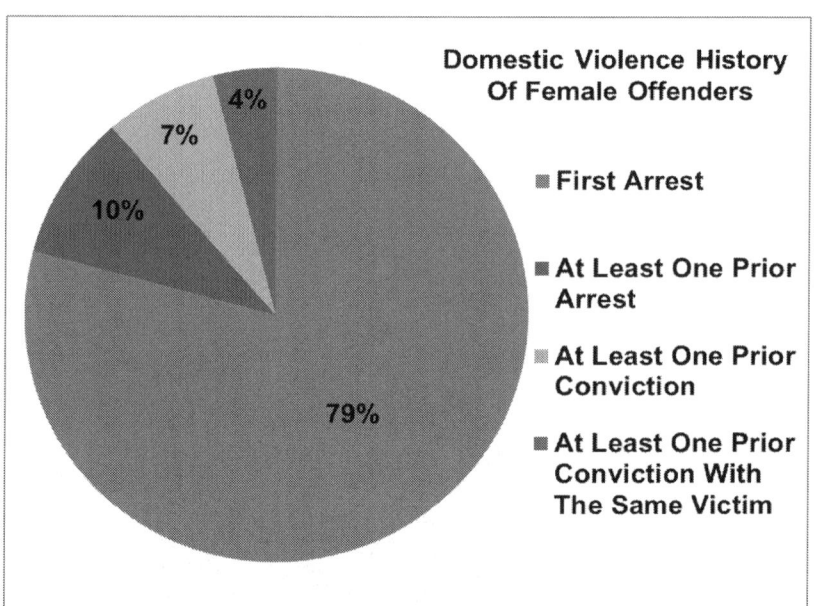

In Shelby County recidivism among male offenders was nearly twice as high as recidivism among female offenders. Forty-one percent of men arrested for domestic violence had prior domestic violence history either in the form of a prior arrest, prior conviction, or prior conviction with the same victim. Twenty-one percent of women arrested for domestic violence had prior domestic violence history. Ideally, what you would like to see is a recidivism rate of 20 percent or less for both men and women. Shelby County's recidivism statistics showed that a large portion of offenders who came into the criminal justice system were not being deterred from future acts of domestic violence, particularly male offenders.

Since youth had been found to be one of the strongest commonalities among offenders in Shelby County, I also looked at the ages of offenders in relation to their prior domestic violence history. Not surprisingly, the data showed that 48 percent of first time offenders were ages 20 to 29. This age range represented the largest age demographic for first time offenders and was in line with other analyses showing youth to be a strong contributing factor of domestic violence.

What was surprising, however, was that 40 percent of repeat offenders were also ages 20 to 29. In other words, many offenders were being arrested and rearrested for domestic violence while they were still in their twenties. The majority of first arrests occurred from ages 20 to 24, and the majority of repeat arrests occurred from ages 25 to 29.

Youth was again found to be a strong commonality among offenders but this time in a different way. Within the age range of 20 to 29, we found the highest offenders (black males); the third highest offenders (black females); the highest number of first time offenders; and the highest number of repeat offenders. The arrest history data provided additional support for activists in Shelby County to focus their preventative efforts on young adults.

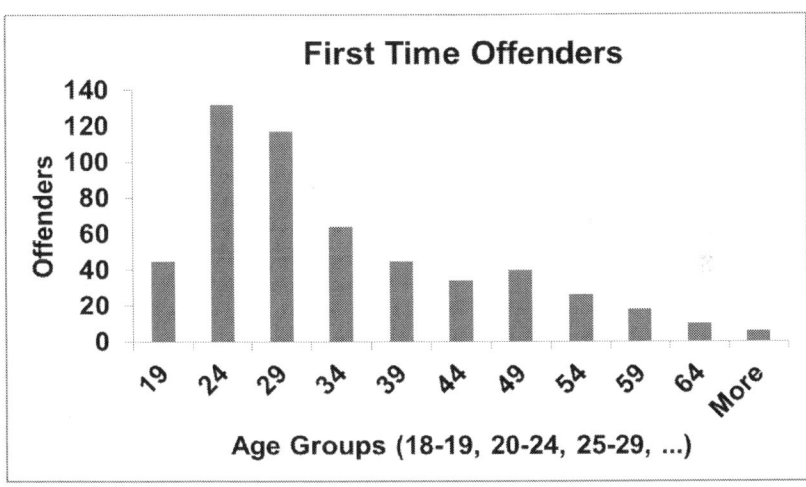

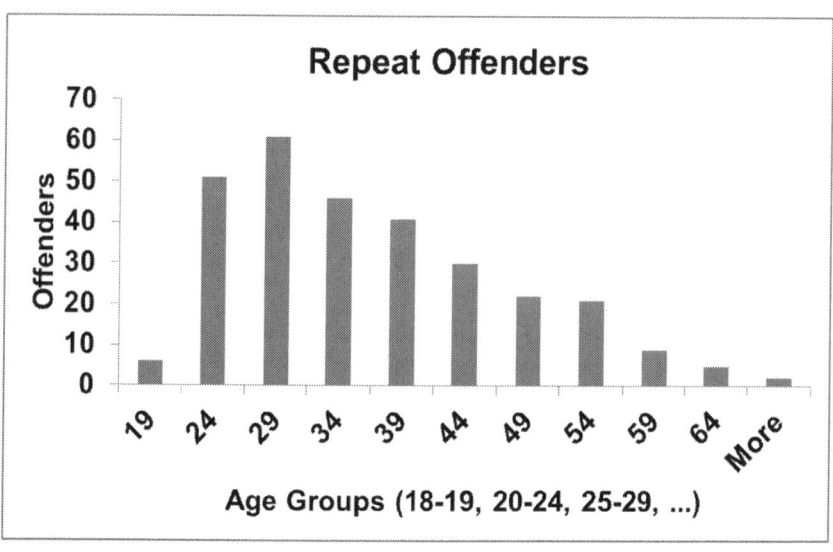

Tactics For Reducing Recidivism

I signed a domestic violence arrest warrant for a young man who had assaulted his girlfriend in her front yard. According to the victim, her boyfriend, who was age 23, was upset because she had allowed another man to drive her home from work. All three worked at the same place, and when her boyfriend came home and found out how she got home, he became irate and started punching her in the face and dragging her on the ground. After the altercation she called the police, and her boyfriend, who had initially left the scene but later came back, was arrested. This was his first domestic violence arrest. The victim was 29 years old.

For Shelby County the case was typical in every way. The offender was a black male in his 20s; he was a first time offender according to his arrest history; his anger was triggered by the victim having an interaction with another man; and he sought to control her behavior by violently assaulting her. Now he was under arrest with an opportunity for the criminal justice system to intervene, levy a punishment, and hopefully stop him from committing future domestic abuse. What could be implemented by the court to change his behavior and keep him from becoming a repeat offender? Jail time? Probation? Batterer intervention program? Anger management classes? Or some combination of all four?

As compelling as these questions are, there is actually a more important question that will largely determine if a court's punitive policies will deter offenders from committing domestic violence in the future. Will the victim assist in the prosecution?

In general, courts have struggled to reduce recidivism despite having an arsenal of punitive measures. Effective solutions to decrease recidivism have been very elusive. The main reason for this is because too many victims fail to follow through with prosecuting offenders. Victims who choose not to participate in the criminal justice process, either by their own choosing or because of coercion from the offender, represent the biggest obstacle for the court in its effort to reduce recidivism. Put simply, if victims do not assist in the prosecution, offenders cannot be sufficiently monitored or effectively prosecuted. Offenders will only receive a slap on the wrist, or even worse, the cases against them will be dismissed. Offenders will then continue to be abusive, having successfully manipulated the victim and the criminal justice system. The problem is so severe that judges handling domestic violence cases need to weigh in and address the problem of reluctant or non-cooperating victims.

Understandably, there may be some judges who think that courts should not get involved with the business of helping to secure a victim's appearance, preferring instead to leave this challenge to prosecutors. I disagree with this thinking and argue that judges must assert themselves in this area because of the unique nature of domestic violence charges. In no other criminal charge do offenders have the ability and means to influence the victim's actions to the extent they do in domestic violence cases. Offenders wield considerable power over victims and routinely use this power to their benefit, particularly when it comes to victims appearing in court. Thus, the playing field is not level when it comes to administering justice in domestic violence cases. Offenders have a heavy advantage from the onset. Because of this, judges should endeavor to make sure that victims have an opportunity to be heard in spite of any duress that may come from offenders.

Speed Up Prosecutions

One possible solution to this dilemma is to speed up the prosecution process and get victims into court as soon as possible. Victims are much more likely to assist in the prosecution when the abuse is fresh in their mind and they see that they are going to get immediate assistance from the court. For domestic violence victims, second thoughts about prosecuting the offender begin to form very quickly, sometimes within hours after an arrest. Courts and prosecutors have to be keenly aware of this and implement procedures aimed at securing the victim's participation right from the beginning of the prosecution.

Specifically, courts should endeavor to involve victims in the criminal justice process immediately after the offender's arrest. Victims should be notified of the offender's first court date and asked to appear in court on that date. Hopefully, the first court date will be the day after an arrest, but it should not be any more than two days later. By getting victims into court on the offender's first court date, the court can accomplish a number of important objectives. First, domestic violence advocates will have an opportunity to speak with victims in person and assess them for any additional services they may need. Additionally, a judge or magistrate will have an opportunity to speak with victims concerning their allegations. This will help the court set appropriate bail and bail conditions. It will also empower victims by giving them an opportunity to be heard by the court or the prosecutor concerning the abuse. Also, prosecutors will have an opportunity to get more detailed information about incidents, take formal statements from victims, preserve any evidence, photograph injuries, and identify any potential witnesses. Last, prosecutors will have an opportunity to obtain accurate contact and emergency contact information for victims. All this becomes possible if victims can get immediate attention from the criminal justice system.

Once an offender obtains counsel, a trial date should be immediately set by the court and communicated to victims. By doing this, victims will know very early in the process exactly when they will have their day in court. Even if the case is resolved without the need for a trial, setting a trial date will let victims know when they will be needed in order to testify against the offender.

Of course, speeding up the criminal justice process will not resolve all the issues that arise from victims failing to cooperate, but an expedited process that gets victims into court quickly will result in a higher percentage of victims participating in the prosecution. When victims participate in the prosecution, courts will have at their disposal a full range of punishment and deterrent options. Courts will have to implement faster procedures in order to secure the victim's participation before reluctance or manipulation from the offender takes hold.

Providing a timely hearing is something I try to be cognizant of when I hear petitions for orders of protection. My goal is to give the petitioner and the respondent a hearing as quickly as possible, usually on the first court date since most people choose to represent themselves. I almost never allow a petition to be reset beyond a second court date, unless both parties agree to a reset. In this way, petitions are decided quickly, victims get the protection they need in a timely fashion, and the parties do not get exasperated with an order of protection process that drags on and requires them to make many court appearances.

Record Victims At The Scene

Whenever possible police officers should use their audio/visual equipment to record what victims say and how they look on the scene. In the same way that officers record DUI suspects, domestic violence victims should be recorded at the time of the incident. What they say about what happened, their physical appearance, injuries, mental state, and overall demeanor should be captured by police, especially when the incident has just recently occurred. By doing this prosecutors will have an alternative way of prosecuting the offender if the victim later becomes uncooperative. The recordings will likely be challenged in court as hearsay; but if the recordings are made while the victim is still under the stress and excitement of the incident, these objections may be overcome. The key is to make these recordings as close in time to the incident as possible. Hopefully, the recordings will not be needed in court, but if they are, prosecutors will have them at their disposal.

Keep Offenders And Victims Separated

Additionally, courts should keep offenders and victims separated for as long as possible. Most offenders are already ordered to stay away from victims when they are released from jail. However, many offenders, sometimes with the acquiescence of the victim, disregard stay-away orders because they are not usually monitored for compliance. The responsibility is placed on the victim to alert the police if the stay-away order is violated by the offender. Usually courts are unaware that the victim and the offender have started living together again, unless there is a subsequent problem which brings the police to the shared residence. The burden to report a violation needs to be removed from victims and placed on the criminal justice system. The failure to monitor stay-away orders is a huge loophole that offenders regularly exploit. It is patently unfair to require victims who are already in a compromised position to report violations.

Courts should consider using global positioning system (GPS) monitoring in the form of ankle bracelets as a condition of release after offenders have been arrested for domestic violence. GPS monitoring could be used to enforce stay-away orders by alerting the police when the offender is at the shared residence or near the victim. In this way, offenders could be immediately rearrested for coming around the victim without the victim's participation. Offenders rearrested for violating a stay-away order would then be subject to an increased or revoked bail which would further drive home a court's intention for the offender to stay away from the victim.

Also, GPS monitoring for purposes of keeping the offender away from the victim should be used as a condition of probation if warranted. If the offender comes to the shared residence while he or she is on probation, the probation administrator should be alerted as to a possible probation violation. Additionally, law enforcement should routinely check on victims to ensure that offenders are in fact staying away from victims. Officers should know the locations of victims who have protective orders in their patrol area. They should then regularly check on victims during their patrols to make sure they are safe and to enforce stay-away orders.

Vigorously fighting to keep offenders away from victims will work to reduce recidivism in several ways. First, it will give the victim a break from the abuser and the abuse. During this time period the victim may decide to part ways with the offender thereby ensuring her long-term safety. Second, prohibiting cohabitation will likely create a hardship for the offender with regard to his or her living arrangements. Such an abrupt disruption in the daily living routine of offenders could deter them from engaging in future domestic abuse, if enforced. Finally, it will send a message to the community that the court is serious about stopping domestic violence.

Victims Affect Recidivism

At first blush, Shelby County's recidivism data seems to suggest that the court needs to get tougher on male, first time offenders. The statistics showed that 41 percent of male offenders had prior domestic violence arrests; and of that number 29 percent had at least one prior domestic violence conviction. This contrasted greatly with the recidivism rate for female offenders which stood at 21 percent. What factors caused this vast difference? Why did male offenders reoffend almost twice as much as female offenders? Why did the court's punitive policies seem to work when the offender was female, but not work when the offender was male?

What this disparity tells us is that prosecution assistance among female victims in Shelby County is very low. Domestic violence prosecutors and courts can only be as tough on offenders as victims allow them to be. If female victims do not follow through with prosecuting, prosecutors cannot be tough on offenders and courts cannot effectively implement policies aimed at deterrence. When offenders are able to get their cases dismissed or are only minimally punished because victims are not participating, the recidivism rate is going to be high.

Domestic Violence Hearsay Exception

There is one solution that would have to be categorized as a potential game-changer in the fight against domestic violence, create an exception to the rule against hearsay for domestic violence testimony. A domestic violence hearsay exception would allow police officers or others to state in court what the victim said about how he or she was abused and by whom. An exception of this nature would have an immediate impact on the state's ability to prosecute offenders effectively and the court's ability to punish guilty offenders sternly. It is a solution that must be given serious consideration because offenders currently have an inherent and unfair advantage over victims.

There are many exceptions to hearsay enumerated in the rules of evidence of any jurisdiction. In general, firmly rooted exceptions have been incorporated for circumstances when statements made outside of court have a high degree of reliability. As a result, these statements are admissible through someone other than the declarant. Additionally, the US Supreme Court has decided that statements made by the declarant during an ongoing emergency can also be admitted through someone other than the declarant. This decision should be enumerated as a hearsay exception that would allow others to testify as to what the victim said while there was an ongoing abuse emergency. With a domestic violence exception conditioned upon concurrency in time with abuse, police officers who arrive at a domestic incident while the altercation is ongoing could later relate to the court what the victim said about abuse, including who inflicted it; a family member contacted during a domestic incident could state to the court what the victim said while abuse was ongoing; or a friend coming to aid a victim during a domestic incident could testify as to what the victim said happened. By creating a hearsay exception of this nature, a great deal of the burden of prosecuting offenders is removed from victims who are inherently subject to duress; and another large loophole that offenders have exploited for years is tightened.

Yet creating this type of exception will likely be met with vigorous opposition. Critics will site the Confrontation Clause of the Sixth Amendment, which states the accused shall have the right to confront the witnesses against him, as the primary reason not to create this exception. This well-established constitutional right helps balance the power between the defendant and the government. Opponents will not want to see this important defense power eroded. Additionally, critics will argue that offenders *should* have their cases dismissed when victims fail to appear in court. Non-appearance suggests the crime did not happen or at the very least there is some mitigating culpability on the part of the victim. Thus, the resulting dismissal is the correct result. Critics will even argue that domestic violence crimes should not be prosecuted any differently than other crimes because the supposed advantage offenders have over victims is not real. Proponents of an exception should expect the arguments against it to be numerous and passionately asserted.

Of course the primary argument in favor of the exception is to create fairness where it currently does not exist and to level the playing field between offenders and victims. The undue influence that offenders regularly impose on victims after they have been arrested can be attested to by thousands of victims and survivors; but there is also another very compelling fairness argument that can be made.

At a judicial commissioners conference I attended in 2012, a judge from Rutherford County, Tennessee told the magistrates it was his usual practice to arrest and bring to court domestic violence victims who failed to appear after being subpoenaed. He reasoned it simply was not fair to demand that police officers risk their lives and personal safety responding to dangerous domestic violence incidents only to have victims fail to assist in the prosecution. He told the magistrates his community would not tolerate police officers failing to show up when there was a domestic incident, so he in turn would not tolerate victims failing to show up to prosecute. To do so would be unfair to police officers who often have to make several domestic calls to the same residence. Many in the room applauded his policy while others remained silent; however, the point he made about fairness to police officers was undeniably true. We ask police officers to intervene into dangerous and unpredictable domestic situations numerous times a day. We then allow offenders to persuade, manipulate, and/or threaten victims into not prosecuting cases. This has the overall effect of decreasing officer safety, particularly when they have to make repeat domestic calls. A domestic violence hearsay exception would allow these officers or others to testify as to what the victim said about abuse if the emergency was ongoing, thus helping to hold offenders accountable for their actions. Once we are able to hold offenders accountable, we will then be able to effectuate a real change in abusive behaviors.

8.

Focus On Offenders

A (Not So) Radical Approach

The idea of focusing on offenders to stem the tide of domestic violence is not new. It is, however, an idea that has not received any significant traction as an effective way to further reduce domestic violence. Usually, attention is paid to offenders only in terms of punitive treatment, while the vast majority of prevention efforts are spent on convincing victims to leave abusive relationships and providing support to those who make this decision.

The harsh reality, however, is that most victims do not want to leave their relationships. Victims want offenders to stop being abusive. They did not fall in love with a person whom they knew was abusive. If at all possible, they want to stay in the relationships in which they have invested so much time, energy, and love. As a result, victims often thwart efforts made by family, friends, activists, prosecutors, and courts to protect them and keep them from being abused. Lack of cooperation from victims continues to stymie progress in reducing domestic violence. It is a frustrating and troubling paradox for those fighting against domestic violence.

Yet victims are right. We should be focusing more of our efforts on getting offenders to change. The question should no longer be *why doesn't she leave?* The question should be *why doesn't he change?* We demand that offenders be punished for the abuses they commit, but we do not demand or expect offenders to stop being abusive. I believe this is a grave oversight in the fight against domestic violence. We have to inundate offenders with anti-domestic violence messages that condemn abuse and teach proper conflict resolution skills. We also have to find ways to increase victim participation in prosecutions so that offenders can be effectively deterred from committing domestic violence in the future.

In deciding to adopt an approach that focuses on offenders and compels them to abandon abusive behaviors, activists should be aware that every community is different. Each community needs to determine exactly who the high offenders are. By doing this, activists will be able to develop targeted preventative tactics that can resonate with high offenders and change abusive behaviors. Additionally, activists will be able to focus their efforts on the offender groups that are causing the most domestic violence in the community. So while focusing on offenders may not be a radical idea, it does represent an intriguing and promising approach to further reduce domestic violence. Furthermore, it is what victims want.

How To Make This Happen In Your Community

In order to implement an offender focused anti-domestic violence campaign in your community, the first step is to ask for it. Call on your community leaders and activists to develop and implement campaigns which target offenders and demand change from them. Most community leaders and activists will already be aware that domestic violence continues to be a significant and serious problem and that efforts to further reduce it have stalled. As a result, if victims, survivors, and concerned citizens create a groundswell of support for campaigns telling offenders to stop being abusive, this call to action will be impossible to ignore. Every time you hear about domestic violence occurring in your community you should reach out to your community leaders and activists and tell them to focus more of their anti-domestic violence efforts on getting offenders to change.

Keep Fighting

In the final analysis, everyone will agree that there is still a considerable amount of work to be done to stop domestic violence. Significant progress has been made over the last 35 years but more work remains. Each year we need to become less and less tolerant of domestic violence while our resolve to eradicate it becomes stronger and stronger. I remain hopeful that domestic violence will become a thing of the past, an ugly part of social history that our children will read about but never have to experience. We can stamp it out completely if we remain diligent, forward thinking, and committed.

Our vision of a world without domestic violence must remain unshakable.

Endnotes

Chapter 1:
· Lieutenant Mark Miller, Homicide Bureau Supervisor, Memphis Police Department.

Chapter 2:
· Criminal Victimization, 1993 – 2011, Bureau of Justice Statistics, U.S. Department of Justice.
· The National Intimate Partner and Sexual Violence Survey (NISVS): 2010 Summary Report, National Center for Injury Prevention and Control, Centers for Disease Control and Prevention, page 39.

Chapter 4:
· It should be noted that within Shelby County there are seven municipalities with Memphis being the largest. The data consists of domestic violence arrests originating in Memphis and unincorporated Shelby County. Domestic violence arrests originating in the other six municipalities are not included in the data.
· Erica L. Smith and Donald J. Farole, Jr., Ph.D., "Profile of Intimate Partner Violence Cases in Large Urban Counties," Bureau of Justice Statistics, U.S. Department of Justice, October 2009.

Chapter 6:
· Division of Violence Prevention, National Center for Injury Prevention and Control, Centers for Disease Control and Prevention.

Chapter 7:
· *Crawford v. Washington*, 541 U.S. 36 (2004); *Davis v. Washington*, 547 U.S. 813 (2006); *Michigan v. Bryant*, 562 U.S. ___ (2011)

About The Author

Judicial Commissioner Kevin Reed is a magistrate of the General Sessions Criminal Court of Shelby County, Tennessee. As a magistrate, he is primarily responsible for setting bonds, reviewing warrants, and presiding over preliminary hearings and petitions for orders of protection in domestic abuse cases. He has worked with victims and offenders of domestic violence for over fifteen years. He received a BS from Massachusetts Institute of Technology and a JD from Howard University School of Law.

He is married to the love of his life, Tamara, and they have two adorable children, Khari and Amara.

Thank you for reading *Focus On Offenders!* Contact me at focusonoffenders@gmail.com. Don't forget to rate and comment on this book.

Made in the USA
Middletown, DE
21 August 2015